"GET AN A

A2 CITIZE

TEXTBOOK AI

DUNCAN HALL

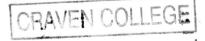

ISBN: 978-1-291-83817-6

Acknowledgements

Thanks to Julia Hall, Virginia Hall and Brian Hall for encouragement, proof-reading, etc. Any mistakes in this book are most definitely my own, but I am indebted to them and others for their assistance. I should also mention Tom, Ben, Eliot, Tami, Rebecca, Olivia, Sameera, Kerry, Charlee and Dan (A2 Citizenship class of 2013/14) Ben, Josh, Beth, Matthew, Simone, Zara, Alex, Frances, Laura, Sonya and Sabrina (from 2012/13) Hannah, Natasha, Joanna and Amreen (from 20011/12) as well as India, Sohail and Ben (from 2010/11).

CONTENTS

INTRODUCTION 7

PART ONE: POWER & JUSTICE 8

1. INTRODUCTION TO CRIME, JUSTICE & PUNISHMENT 8

2. WHAT IS CRIME? 10

    a. Defining crime 10

    b. Who commits crime and why? 12

    c. Theories of crime 15

3. THE CRIMINAL JUSTICE SYSTEM 19

    a. The Police 19

    b. The Crown Prosecution Service 20

    c. Criminal Law and Criminal Trials 21

    d. Judges & Juries 24

    e. Sentencing 26
    f. Miscarriages of Justice 28

4. INTRODUCTION TO POLITICS, POWER AND PARTICIPATION 30

5. REPRESENTATIVE DEMOCRACY 30

    a. Indirect and Direct Democracy 30

    b. Elections in the UK 31

   c. UK Electoral Systems   *32*

   d. Our Representatives   *41*

   e. Citizen Participation   *43*

6. PARLIAMENT & GOVERNMENT   *45*

   a. UK Political Parties & Ideologies   *45*

   b. The Powers of Parliament   *49*

   c. The Powers of the Prime Minister   *50*

7. BRITAIN IN THE WORLD   *52*

   a. Britain in the European Union   *52*

   b. Britain and other international   *56*
      organisations

   c. Globalisation and Politics   *58*

PART TWO: GLOBAL ISSUES & MAKING A   *61*
DIFFERENCE

1. INTRODUCTION TO GLOBAL CITIZENSHIP   *61*

2. HUMAN RIGHTS   *61*

3. CONFLICT & CONFLICT RESOLUTION   *66*

   a. Northern Ireland   *67*

   b. Iraq   *69*

   c. Afghanistan   *72*

    d. Syria   74

    e. Ukraine   75
4. THE ENVIRONMENT   76

5. TRADE & GLOBALISATION   78

6. ACTIVE CITIZENSHIP: "HOW TO" GUIDE   83

GLOSSARY   85
MODEL ANSWER PLANS   93

INTRODUCTION

Welcome to the A2 Citizenship Studies book "Get an A" Guide. As you will know by now, Citizenship is a synoptic, interdisciplinary A Level through which you should demonstrate your awareness of a number of related subject areas (e.g. Government & Politics, Law, Sociology, etc.), your general knowledge of the world around you and – perhaps most importantly – your ability to construct an argument and communicate your ideas. As such, a textbook and revision guide can only give an overview of the topic areas covered by the specification and point you in the right direction for further amplification. This should work in conjunction with the support from your tutor and the resources available from AQA's own website.

Furthermore, a significant part of A2 Citizenship Studies is on a topic unknown to students, teachers and textbook-writers until the academic year is well under way! Pre-release material will be sent to your college or school and additional resources made available to your teachers from the exam board. However, for that section of the A2, this book can only give general advice on how to tackle the questions and examples of the *sort* of topic that might come up. I would also strongly advise looking at past papers on the AQA website to assist with this.

    This further illustrates the point that a large part of the assessment for this subject is not so much *what* you know, but what you do with what you know. Learning the subject content in this book is only one ingredient to "getting an A", and indeed candidates who know only a fraction of the content included here may well get their A grades if they construct good essays, evaluate material effectively and generally perform to their best. As such, there are plenty of exam tips in here too.

It is essential that Citizenship students, especially at A2, keep a close eye on current affairs and the news. Some of the examples outlined in this book are quite up-to-date at the time of writing, but some stories move very quickly indeed.

Exam-style questions and model answers in this book are based on the style of AQA exam questions and related directly to the specification; however, should any be the same as past or future exam papers, specimen papers or mark schemes, this is entirely coincidental.

PART ONE: POWER & JUSTICE

INTRODUCTION TO CRIME, JUSTICE AND PUNISHMENT

To perform well in this part of Unit 3, you need a broad overview of Criminal Law, knowledge of some useful examples, and also an overview of some sociological approaches to criminology. Law students will be at some advantage in this module, as will Sociology students who have studied a Crime & Deviance module. However, while Citizenship candidates will always be rewarded for bringing in relevant knowledge from other disciplines, the necessary content for success in this module is not so expansive and complex that students who do not cover these matters in other A Levels cannot achieve the highest grades.

You should know:

- Problems with defining crime and some theory relating to this, as well as theories relating to crime statistics and apparent trends in offending
- The way crimes are investigated and brought to trial, including the powers of the police and the role of the CPS
- The different types of criminal trial, when and how these work
- The role of judge and jury and issues relating to sentencing and punishment
- Useful examples to illustrate aspects of all the above

Confidence in these areas will allow you to answer Crime, Justice and Punishment questions with relative ease. It is also worth considering what your *opinion* is of some of these issues, as well as understanding the opinions of others. So *do* spend some time considering whether you think the police have too many powers or too few, whether sentences are too harsh or too lenient and exactly what the purpose of punishment is. The ability to debate these sorts of questions, rationally and with evidence to back up your views, will be of enormous value when it comes to writing coherent and persuasive essays on these sorts of subjects.

In Citizenship Studies, perhaps more than in any other subject, you will be rewarded for successfully arguing your view in the essay. Of course, when doing this, you do need to take care that your view *is* rational, and *can* be backed up by examples and evidence *and* that you properly take account of alternative views. For example, if you believe that the death penalty should be reintroduced for some offences, you are *allowed* to make that argument and, of course, you could point to some emotive, extreme offences where many people might share your view that the perpetrator should have been executed. However, you would need to show an awareness of why we no longer have the death penalty (including the role of the Human Rights Act) and also an understanding of some of the counter-arguments, including issues relating to miscarriages of justice and people who either *were* executed and shouldn't have been (e.g. Derek Bentley – why not research this example on the internet?) and those who it is likely would have been executed had we still had the death penalty and actually had been wrongly convicted (e.g. the Guildford Four – research this example too, or watch the film *In the Name of the Father*.)

You should also include some of your knowledge from AS Citizenship in this unit: your broad understanding of the differences between civil and criminal law, the role of solicitors, barristers and the courts and the nature of the British legal system, learnt in Unit 1, will be of enormous use here.

WHAT IS CRIME?

A. Defining crime

It might seem very obvious to us what a crime is. Write your own definition before reading another word!

If you said something along the lines of "any act that breaks the law" then you are certainly along the right lines!

In the British legal system, a crime requires *actus reus* and *mens rea*. These latin phrases mean "guilty act" and "guilty mind". What this means is that, for a jury to find somebody guilty of a crime they must be satisfied that they both committed the act, *and* intended to do so. This latter point can, of course, be very subjective and difficult to prove. Is intent there if the perpetrator has a mental illness? What if somebody had intended to commit a lesser crime and "accidentally" committed a worse one (e.g. an assault causing somebody's death)?

"Any act that breaks the law" includes things like breaking the speed limit, illegally downloading music from the internet, and drinking/smoking/having sex under age. It is perhaps not stretching the imagination to suggest that some people in your Citizenship class will have committed one or more of these offences at some time. Does this make them *criminals*?

What about people who broke laws that have since been abolished or changed? What about people who break entirely irrational or bizarre laws? For example, it is illegal to die in the Houses of Parliament (there is some debate about this; it could be one of those facts that loses a lot of marks on "QI"). Several MPs over the years have died in Parliament but have not been declared dead until arriving at a hospital to avoid this odd legal legacy (e.g. Airey Neave who was killed by the IRA).

On this basis we might take the view that there is a difference between things that we consider to be *wrong* and things that are criminal. It might be that some things are *illegal* that we consider justifiable or acceptable and that there are other things that we consider *wrong* or *immoral* that are, nevertheless *legal*.

Make two lists: Illegal but justifiable; Legal but immoral

If possible compare your lists with those of somebody else and have a bit of an argument about them! It is likely that you have some disagreements. (e.g. one person might argue that some illegal drug taking is acceptable whereas another person may feel very strongly that it isn't; religious beliefs might lead to some quite strongly opposing views on some of these matters, as might strong views on issues such as animal rights).

Of course, some of the most important changes and advances in society were achieved by people breaking the law: Nelson Mandela, Gandhi, the Suffragettes, civil rights protesters in the US, Resistance movements against Nazism. They all broke laws; they were all – technically at least – criminal. However, the world is a much better place for them, and their law-breaking was of fundamental importance to their achievements.

However...

Make another list, this time: Criminal and Immoral

It is likely this list is longer than the previous ones and includes many of the key criminal acts that we most associate with criminal law: murder, rape, assault, theft, robbery, etc. As such, while it is important to understand that there might be *unjust laws* and there are situations where *civil disobedience* is justified, criminal law and the criminal justice system are of enormous importance to maintaining a civil society and protecting the population.

It is not quite so simple as to say that a crime is anything that breaks the law. Some things that are illegal are *civil* matters rather than criminal ones (that is, people are found to be liable or not liable rather than guilty or not guilty, and the defendant would have to pay money rather than serve a sentence – e.g. it is against the law to slander or libel somebody but it is not, technically, a crime).

So which crimes are the worst? Why? Discuss this with your peers and justify your answers. Is mugging worse than fraud? Murder worse than war crimes?

Before we move on, make sure you have in your notes:

- A definition of crime, including some consideration of problems associated with crime

- A quick overview of the difference between criminal and civil law from AS Citizenship

- Examples of laws that are regularly broken

- Examples of social, legal or political changes that have come about because of law-breakers

B. Who commits crime and why?

So who are the criminals then? Official crime statistics appear to help us here: apparently criminals are likely to be men, they're likely to be young, they're likely to live in urban areas, be working-class and disproportionately from minority ethnic backgrounds. So, some very important questions: do the statistics reflect reality? And if they do, what reasons might there be to explain these apparent trends? To put it crudely, why is a young, working-class urban black man more likely to commit crime than a middle-aged, middle-class, rural white woman?

Go to http://www.statistics.org.uk and look at crime statistics for the area where you live. Can you spot any trends? Are there any surprising figures for your local community? Can you account for them

First of all, the sociologists among you will know that you should always be wary of statistics. They are not a direct reflection of reality – they have been created by people, for a purpose. The data included has been collected in a particular way. In the case of crime statistics, the main official source is from the police, and relates to the reporting of crime, detection of crime and prosecution of criminals. *Police statistics* are supplemented by the *British Crime Survey* which is what is known as a *victim survey* – a large sample of members of the public are asked what crimes they have been victims of that year.

Both sets of data might miss an awful lot of crime.

Let's take the police statistics first. Most of the crimes that the police come to know about are *reported* to them. Therefore, one set of crimes not included here are *unreported crimes*. That means that there will be a disproportionate number of *property crimes* in the statistics, because people will often report a robbery because of any associated insurance claims. They are perhaps less likely to report a traffic offence or minor cases of assault.

Why might people choose not to report a crime? Have you ever been a victim of a crime that you then chose not to report?

A significant minority of crimes investigated by the police (and therefore finding their way into official police statistics) are crimes directly observed or detected by the police themselves, rather than reported to them by members of the public. These crimes, of course, are overwhelmingly detected where there is a concentration of police resources. In areas regularly patrolled by the police or with a high police presence, far more crimes are likely to be detected or observed than in areas where the police are rarely seen. As such, it is not surprising that statistics find a higher concentration of crime in some urban settings than in a remote village.

Of course, the police concentrate their resources on specific areas for a number of reasons, one of which is an analysis of their statistics, which does produce a rather circular argument: which came first, the high crime rate or the high police presence?

Other issues relating to this question are more controversial. One key one is the issue of *police discretion* and whether this might be driven by prejudice.

The famous *McPherson Report* of 1999, into the police investigation of the murder of black teenager Stephen Lawrence in 1993, concluded that the Metropolitan Police was *"institutionally racist"*. Subsequent investigations, including a BBC report *The Secret Policeman* found shocking evidence of racism in other UK forces too. In the latter programme, a police cadet openly admits to using his discretion in a blatantly racist manner, charging black or Asian drivers for motoring offences on the same day as turning a blind eye to the same offence carried out by a white woman. Another cadet talked of stopping and searching any car with two or more black or Asian people in it, simply on the grounds of their race. If such approaches were happening across the country, even by a small minority of officers, it could significantly impact on police statistics.

Then there is the issue of wealthy criminals. There is some evidence, even in the recent Leveson Inquiry which (along with other things) looked at the relationship between the police and the media, that those with power and influence might be able to "buy off" the police and avoid investigation and detection.

So we've raised questions about the statistics in relation to *location*, *ethnicity* and *class*. What about *gender*?

One theory is the *chivalry thesis*. This argument suggests that law enforcement officers are often men and they will often be more lenient with female offenders than male offenders out of gentlemanliness! *Does this sound likely?* Associated with this is a broader idea that society expects a degree of criminality among men, but is shocked when women commit crimes (because of social and gender norms). As such, women will often be considered less culpable for their crimes (they were led astray by a male accomplice for example, or they were out of their mind). As it happens, some research of female offenders shows that quite a high percentage of them *did* have a controlling male accomplice.

A very controversial (and frankly rather ridiculous) theory for why women appear to commit fewer crimes than men is that put forward by Otto Pollack. *(One way to commit this theory to memory is to think: Otto Pollack – Utter Bollocks).* He argued that women do commit as many crimes as men but they are naturally better at hiding it and are naturally better liars. His "proof" of this comes from women hiding menstruation and "faking orgasms". I include this because, if nothing else, you're likely to remember it! But it is a discredited theory today, I'm pleased to say!

Of course, other theories relating to gender and crime seek to explain why it is that women might *actually* commit fewer crimes than men, not just appear to in the statistics. The "sex role" theories vary from those that see women as being *biologically* more caring and nurturing than men because of their role as mothers, and those that see girls being taught to be more caring and nurturing through gender socialisation. The feminist, Frances Heidensohn, argues that women are more controlled throughout their lives and therefore have fewer "opportunities" to deviate. She argues that girls are more controlled by their families than boys, until they marry and are then controlled by their husbands. As a lot of crime might be carried out by people out late and on their own, fewer women and girls fit into that category than men. She calls this *control theory.* Another associated feminist theory is *marginalisation theory* which suggests that women do not have the "opportunities" to commit crimes because they are marginalised in society through carrying out a domestic role. The argument points to the fact that crimes are also often carried out through work and, until relatively recently, women were excluded from the workplace to a large extent.

These theories might go some way to explain why the statistics show that there has been an *increase* in female crime in the last twenty to thirty years, especially in occupational crime (crime at work) and anti-social behaviour.

Just as there are theories to explain why women might actually commit fewer crimes than men (and therefore the statistics might not be too misleading) there are also many theories that seek to explain working-class crime and crime by minority ethnic offenders, as we shall consider in the next section.

In 2014, the Office for National Statistics (ONS) removed their "gold standard" rating from police statistics on the grounds that they are unreliable. A parliamentary committee even accused the police of deliberately misrecording crime in order to meet targets. As such, while police statistics are still availible, the ONS now only recommend British Crime Survey data as national statistics.

Why might victim surveys like the British Crime Survey produce misleading statistics? They certainly reveal a vast array of crimes that police statistics miss: those crimes that, for whatever reason, we chose not to report or that the police did not consider matters worth pursuing. But they can still be misleading.

First of all, "victimless" crimes are missing. Many crimes have no victim, no immediate victim, or the victims are broadly diffused among a great many people. These will not appear in the statistics. Many traffic offences and drug-related offences, for example, will be missing. So will some cases of fraud and other *"white-collar crime"*. There will still be some crimes that, just as the victim did not want to speak about them to the police, they would not want to speak about them to a Home Office researcher either. (These might include crimes involving family members, personal or "embarrassing" crimes, etc.)

Then, of course, people do not always remember things quite correctly, or might amend events for the researcher, deliberately or unconsciously. For example, when somebody knows *nothing* about the perpetrator of a crime, they often still imagine somebody. That imagined somebody might well fit many of the stereotypes we mentioned at the start of this section. Some months after the offence, that imagined perpetrator might well have "turned into" a real person: therefore a young black man might well be recorded as having committed a crime when in fact the victim never saw the perpetrator at all.

For all these reasons, we do have to be very careful when we look at crime statistics. They can be helpful, but they only give a partial picture. Some researchers have also used "self-report studies" where people are asked about the crimes they have *committed*. Although this gives a more detailed picture of minor offences that is missing from both the police statistics and the British Crime Survey, few people would "self-report" serious crimes, so it tends to be an overview of some "anti-social behaviour" and, therefore, a partial picture once again.

In Summary

Official Police Statistics	British Crime Survey
<ul><li>Criticised for a being a *social construct* rather than a *social fact*</li><li>Reflect *police priorities*</li><li>Only include reported/recorded crime</li><li>Changes over time can be misleading (e.g. categories and methods of collection change)</li><li>Could be politcally manipulated</li></ul>	<ul><li>Includes many unreported crimes missing from the official police statistics</li><li>People's recollections might be faulty</li><li>Doesn't include "victimless crimes"</li></ul>

C. Theories of crime

While not necessarily essential for success in this module, an overview of some sociological theories of crime would certainly be helpful.

Subcultural Theories

A number of sociological theories of crime are often grouped together as "subcultural theories" because they are based on the idea that there are small groups in society that have norms and values that differ from that of "mainstream" society. They are influenced by a classic American theory (itself not a subcultural theory): *strain theory* by Robert Merton. His basic idea was that it was normal in society to want to have wealth, comfort and "the American dream" and that there was a socially acceptable way to reach it: work hard, get qualifications, etc. However, for some there was a *strain* between the goals and their ability to attain them. He argued that there were various possible adaptations people make, relating to goals and means – some people conform but others "innovate" (achieve wealth by criminal actions) or "retreat" (drop out of it altogether).

This can cause crime among some groups in society.

Some key subcultural theories are:
        i)   Cloward and Ohlin (illegitimate opportunity structures)
        ii) Albert Cohen (status frustration)
        iii) Walter Miller (focal concerns)

A key critique of subcultural theories comes from *Matza (subterranean values)*.

> Web task:
> Research the basic outline of each of these theories and find strengths/weaknesses of each of them.
> Why not start a Citizenship blog (there are lots of "blogging" platforms online that you could use) and summarize these theories in your first blogpost?

Labelling Theory

A different sociological theory of crime/deviance is Howard Becker's "Labelling Theory" based on his central argument that "deviant behaviour is behaviour that people so label". This is quite an important difference from what we've said about criminal/deviant acts so far. Becker is saying that the only thing that deviant acts have in common is that other people describe them as deviant.

As such Becker is a lot more interested in the *"societal reaction"* to deviance in the media or by law enforcement groups, rather than the deviant acts themselves. It leads to other interesting ideas such as *deviancy amplification* and *moral panics* and *folk devils*.

Deviancy Amplification refers to the idea that the reaction to deviant behaviour can actually make the behaviour worse or increase it. An example might be that media interest in knife crime can lead to more people carrying knives (because they think everybody else is doing it). A famous example comes from Stanley Cohen and his research into *Folk Devils and Moral Panics*. He studied fights between "mods" and "rockers" in Brighton in the 1960s and particularly the media response to them. He concluded that the clashing youths were turned into "folk devils" and prompted a "moral panic" in the media. In other words, young people were not especially scary and violent and there was not really an explosion of trouble: the media fury was not reflecting reality. However, as a result of the media interest, more and more people went to Brighton to see what all the fuss was about, and to get in the newspapers and on the news. Cohen concluded that the media essentially created the social problem it was reporting on.

Marxist Theories

Marxist criminologists have tended to focus on questions about who makes the laws and why. For Marxists, the laws are made by the bourgeoisie (the ruling class) in their own interests, and against the interests of the proletariat (the working class). An example of this would be laws on trespass which clearly serve the interest of those who own land against those who do not. For this reason, Marxists argue that it is unsurprising that working-class people are over-represented in the crime statistics as the whole purpose of the criminal justice system is to control the working class. They point to things that rich people do that (from their perspective) are clearly wrong but are (or were at the time they were writing) legal: low pay, disregard for workers' health and safety, tax avoidance, etc. As such they are interested in *corporate crime* (crime committed by companies) and *white collar crime* (crime committed by middle-class people) and point to the fact that sentences for such crimes are often shorter, if anybody is convicted at all. Some neo-Marxists, like Stuart Hall, have argued that some of the issues raised by labelling theory (above) also relate to Marxist ideas as the ruling class might deliberately create a moral panic in order to distract people from other things that are happening. Stuart Hall argued that a *moral panic* about black muggers in the 1970s was designed to distract people from economic crisis and ensure that working class people turned on each other rather than aim their anger or concerns at the ruling class.

In the 1980s some criminologists, both left wing and right wing, were concerned that most existing criminological theory was just too *theoretical*. Crime might be caused by subcultures, or by class exploitation, or by media labelling, but none of that helps the victims of crime. Crime is a very real *problem* for lots of people. The result of this focus was *left realism* and *right realism*. Left Realists (some of whom were previously considered to be Marxists or Neo-Marxists) essentially embraced that famous Tony Blair idea "tough on crime, tough on the causes of crime". They argued that poverty, relative deprivation and social problems were causes of crime and therefore social policies needed to be introduced to tackle these problems. But they were quick to point out that while traditional Marxist views almost seemed to present the criminals as the victims, in fact the *victims* of crime were also most likely to be working class, and therefore people with left-wing views should focus on preventing crime not almost seeming to excuse it. On the other side of the fence, the Right Realists pushed for *zero-tolerance policies*. They argued that a society that tolerated small amounts of anti-social behaviour will become plagued with crime. A neighbourhood where broken windows are left unrepaired will soon be overcome with other forms of crime, because it's clear that there is a lack of community cohesion and respect. Just as left realism could be seen to influence the criminal justice policies of New Labour, right realism has also been influential on real social policy (e.g. in New York under mayor Rudy Giuliani where various "zero-tolerance" schemes were experimented with). These were generally successful (crime rates in New York fell sharply) although critics pointed to people serving custodial sentences for minor or trivial crimes, and also to a large rise in complaints against the police. Left Realists argue for more *community policing* to improve the relations between the communities and those who police them, whereas Right Realists suggest a much "tougher" approach, criticised by the leftwingers as being "military-style" conflict policing.

It would be useful to have a general overview of these theories so that you could bring them into an essay and use them on different sides of an argument.

Test Yourself:

1. What is the British Crime Survey?
2. Which criminologists favour a "zero tolerance" approach to crime?
3. What was Tony Blair's slogan about crime?
4. Name a subcultural theory of crime
5. Give a real historical example of criminal behaviour that is generally admired
6. Give a current example of something which most people think is wrong but is not illegal

THE CRIMINAL JUSTICE SYSTEM

A. The police

When a crime has been committed the police become involved either because a member of the public *reported* the crime or because a police officer themselves *observed* or *detected* the crime. The vast majority of cases will be as a result of reports from the public. There then follows a police investigation. The precise procedure will depend on the nature of the offence, but usually evidence will be collected at the scene (like in CSI!) and statements will be taken from witnesses.

A number of rules constrain the police when it comes to the collection of evidence and the taking of statements / conducting of interviews. The reasons for these restraints are to try and prevent some of the miscarriages of justice that have occurred in the past and are the subject of a later section.

The police can use a range of statutory powers to help them in their investigation, including the powers to: stop and search; search a property; power of arrest; power to detain the suspect; power to interview suspect on tape; power to interview a witness; power to take fingerprints and intimate or non-intimate samples (including DNA samples); power to convene an identification procedure (e.g. identity parade).

When the police arrest a suspect, his or her rights are read to them. The form of words used today is:

"You do not have to say anything. However, it may harm your defence if you do not mention when questioned something which you later rely on in court. Anything you do say may be given in evidence."

While a suspect is being questioned, they are entitled to have a legal adviser present to ensure that rights are respected by the police (under the Police and Criminal Evidence Act, 1984). Access to the duty solicitor at the police station is free of charge. Some suspects will choose to employ a different solicitor, perhaps one whom they regularly use.

The police can hold a suspect for up to **24 hours** before they have to *charge* them or release them. In the case of serious crime this can be extended to **96 hours** or, if arrested under the Prevention of Terrorism Act, **14 days**.

The decision on whether to charge the suspect is taken by the Crown Prosecution Service.

B. The Crown Prosecution Service (CPS)

- The Crown Prosecution Service (CPS) makes the decision to charge based on the evidence put forward by the police investigation

- Where a decision is taken to charge the suspect, a "charge sheet" will be issued to the suspect detailing all the "information" on which the defendant will be tried

- The Charge Sheet will include the date of the first appearance before a magistrates court

- The defendant might be kept in custody until that date or released on police bail (depending on the seriousness of the offence)

- Police bail can also be used when the police need to continue their investigation to satisfy the CPS

The CPS then conducts the case of the prosecution in any ensuing court case.

When the CPS makes the decision about whether to charge a suspect they have to consider a few factors. The most important factor is the likelihood of conviction. As well as being lawyers, they are custodians of public money and it is important that they do not waste the time of the court or the money of the taxpayer. Therefore they need to be clear that the evidence that the police have gathered is, in their view, robust enough to ensure a conviction. Where police evidence is poor, a judge can be very critical of the CPS. They also need to take a decision as to whether a conviction is in the public interest. For example, they might conclude that the misdemeanor is too minor to justify the expenditure.

C. Criminal Law and criminal trials

Once a decision has been taken to prosecute a suspect, they go to *trial*. Not all offences are tried in the same way, in the UK. There are *summary*, *indictable* and *either-way* offences, and each are dealt with differently.

Prosecuting a summary offence

A summary offence is one which is considered relatively minor and is therefore to be tried swiftly and without the need for a full jury trial. Sometimes with minor summary offences, an individual is not charged at the police station and instead the magistrates court issues a summons. The summons includes the date of the hearing before the magistrates court (an example when this might be used is non-payment of council tax)

The process for all summary trials is as follows:

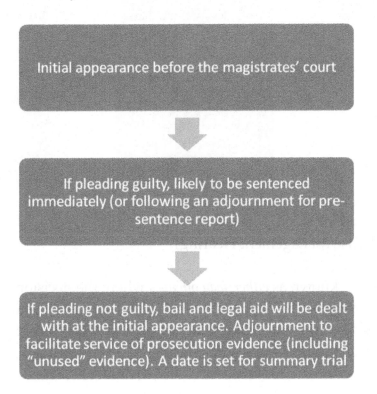

Initial appearance before the magistrates' court

If pleading guilty, likely to be sentenced immediately (or following an adjournment for pre-sentence report)

If pleading not guilty, bail and legal aid will be dealt with at the initial appearance. Adjournment to facilitate service of prosecution evidence (including "unused" evidence). A date is set for summary trial

Prosecuting an idictable offence

An indictable offence is one which is considered sufficiently serious to require a full jury trial and cannot be dealt with swiftly in the magistrates court.

The process is as follows:

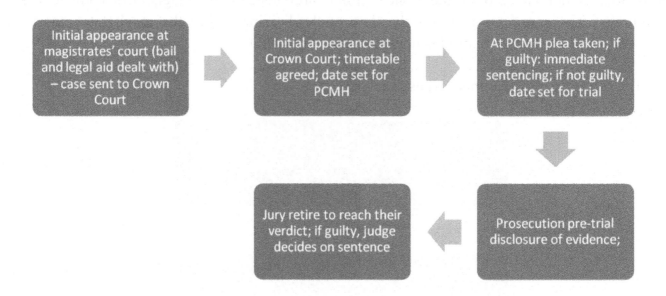

(PCMH = Plea and Case Management Hearing)

There are also offences known as *either-way offences* where the decision on whether to hear the case summarily in the magistrates court or to indict the defendant and have a full jury trial depends on how the trial develops. These tend to be for offences that are mid-way between summary and indictable in terms of their seriousness.

The process in these cases is:

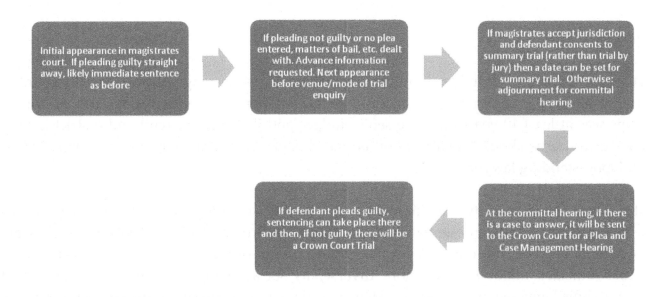

In a summary case, appeals against conviction and/or sentence will usually be heard in the Crown Court (if it is against conviction there will be a full rehearing of the case). Appeals against conviction and/or sentence from the Crown Court are heard by the Court of Appeal. Leave to appeal must be sought (this can be granted by the trial judge).

Remember *judges* are legal professionals (described in the next section) whereas magistrates are *lay people*.

Do some research into how somebody becomes a magistrate. What training do they undertake? Why should some crimes be heard by lay magistrates rather than professional judges? What is your opinion? Include this in your notes.

D. Judges & Juries

Judges

There are a wide range of judges in the UK, reflecting the wide range of courts in the country. What they all have in common is a number of years' experience as a solicitor or barrister. In the past this was at least 10 years for more senior judges and 7 years for circuit and district judges. Because of concerns about the *diversity* of judges, this has been changed, although most judges are still long-standing lawyers.

This issue about diversity is an important one. A criticism of the judiciary over the years has been that it is not at all representative of the people of Britain. To put it bluntly, judges are overwhelmingly white, middle or upper-class, middle-aged or older men. The hope is that over time the judiciary might become more diverse, as social changes mean more female and minority-ethnic lawyers become judges. However, the law remains an exclusive profession. Go to the websites of a random selection of law firms and look at the photographs of the partners. I am sure you will see the occasional woman and non-white face, but it really is still dominated by middle-aged white men. The class issue is even harder to tackle as whatever somebody's social origins, the education and professional background required to become a judge is one that can only reasonably be described as middle class or above. Of course, we would not want judges *not* to have law degrees, so it is perhaps a problem that cannot be resolved.

The inevitability of at least some exclusivity in the judiciary is one of the many arguments for why we are tried before a *jury* of our peers.

Juries

Any of us might be called for jury duty at some point, provided we are on the electoral register and are not in prison! Indeed, we might be called more than once. A panel is selected and then 12 of them are called at random for each trial. Occasionally jurors may be deemed unsuitable because of having very little English or because of profound disability. It is possible to get out of jury service in some circumstances (e.g. you have already booked a wedding or holiday, have been called to jury service in the last two years, have something particularly pressing at work).

There are questions about whether trial by jury is an important right and civil liberty, or in fact an anachronism that does not really ensure justice is done. In the deep South of the USA in the early and mid 20th century, all-white juries effectively worked hand-in-hand with lynch mobs to ensure that those who killed black people were acquitted and that black suspects were found guilty. (The juries were all-white because of restrictions on who could register to vote in many US states). Juries are not lawyers, and often court cases hang on rather complex questions of law – *not* on the gut instinct of whether people feel the defendant is guilty or not. A recent example which has raised further questions about trial by jury was the case of former cabinet minister Chris Huhne and his wife Vicky Pryce where, eventually, the judge felt the need to dismiss a jury because they seemed to demonstrate such a profound lack of understanding of the task that they had been set. In this case the jury asked a number of quite odd questions to the judge for clarification before reaching their verdict. These included whether Vicky Pryce's wedding vows (to "obey" her husband) meant that, as he had told her to take his speeding points, she could not really be considered guilty if she had religious convictions. This had not been Vicky Pryce's defence so was, at best, an odd question. They also asked for the judge to define "reasonable doubt". (His helpful response was "doubt that is reasonable"). Perhaps most bizarrely, they asked if they could reach a verdict based on material that was not presented to the court and had no facts or evidence to support it... Critics of jury service point to the fact that at least this jury asked the questions, perhaps others merely reach their verdicts with just as shaky an understanding of their task.

However, the defenders of jury service would argue that the discussion between twelve people can reach a considered, fair and sensible judgement, whereas a single judge cannot help but be subjective, for all his (and it probably *is* a him) knowledge of the law. There have been several studies into judges in the UK that conclude that they are often *out of touch* with modern society and, as such, might arrive at equally unreasonable conclusions to those of some jurors. While some jurors might be ignorant of the law, some judges are ignorant of modern society. It is still the case that most judges went to public school, most went to Oxford or Cambridge and the vast majority are men. In the past a judge dismissed a case against an alleged ticket tout because he was unaware that Arsenal was a premiership football team. There have been many outrageously sexist comments by judges in court (e.g. "if a woman upsets you that's part of their function in life – the fun they have") as well as racist comments. Some of the most serious examples of this problem have related to sexual offences. Two examples in the 1990s, for example, were when a man was given a short sentence for rape (3 and a half years) and the judge's explanation was that the man and the woman knew each other and this was not, in his view, "the more serious type of rape". Another judge (in his 70s) put a man on two years' probation for the attempted rape of an 8 year old girl, commenting that he was convinced that the girl "was no angel" (an appeals court later criticised this judgement and gave the man four months in prison, which still appears very lenient.) There are other famous cases where judges have questioned whether a woman could have been raped if she became pregnant after the incident or have made reference to the clothes that the victims were wearing. Only last year a judge referred to an 11-year-old rape victim as a "willing participant" and, as such, gave a more lenient sentence to the two rapists than he otherwise might have done.

So there is a big debate – should we still use juries to reach the verdict in criminal trials despite evidence of flaws and miscarriages of justice? Is there more that can be done to ensure that judges have a better understanding of modern society and do not bring their prejudices or biased views to court with them?

Make a poster summarizing the arguments for and against Trial by Jury

E. Sentencing

So judges (and magistrates in lesser cases) choose sentences, within guidelines set down by the government. In this section we will consider the different types of sentence available and what factors judges and magistrates might take into account. But it is also a good opportunity to think about *punishment* more generally. What is the purpose of punishment? It is this fundamental question that underpins debates about sentencing.

So: why do we punish?

- Retribution
- Compensation of victim
- Prevention of further crimes
- Deterrence
- Rehabilitation

It is likely that there will be a range of views within your Citizenship class as to which of these is most important. It is also likely that you will feel that the nature of the crime committed, and perhaps the motive of the criminal or the circumstances in which the crime was committed, is also important when evaluating these purposes of punishment.

If we consider somebody found guilty of a cold-blooded, pre-meditated murder and somebody found guilty of possessing class A drugs, the latter being an addict, it is likely that different punishments, and different purposes for punishment, would come to mind.

In the former case our primary concerns are likely to be: justice for the victim and family of the victim and ensuring the safety of the public. In the second case we might be tempted to see the criminal as themselves a sort of victim. Rehabilitiation will come much more to the fore. Some of us might also think that deterring others from taking drugs might also be a factor in choosing a proper punishment.

Here are a few short fictional scenarios. Decide for yourself what a just and proper punishment might be for each "criminal". Be prepared to defend your decision against your classmates who may consider you to have been either too soft or too harsh.

Scenario A: A woman has been found guilty of manslaughter. She killed her abusive husband after five years of sustained physical and mental abuse. Her act was pre-meditated. She spiked his drink and then battered him to death with a cricket bat once he was unconscious. Her initial story to the police was that there had been a break-in but she later admitted what she had done, pleading "guilty" to manslaughter but "innocent" of murder, in court.

Scenario B: A well-known pop singer has been found guilty of possession of a Class A substance (crack cocaine), with intent to supply. In his defence, he claimed that the significant amount was only for his personal use, but witnesses testified that he regularly shared drugs with young, impressionable fans. A music magazine recently declared the singer a "21ˢᵗ century icon".

Scenario C: An 18-year-old heroin addict has been found guilty of shoplifting. The unemployed girl stole £600 worth of clothes from a high street store with the intention of selling the items on, to raise money to support her addiction.

Scenario D: A 17-year old student has been found guilty of rape, after getting his 15-year-old girlfriend pregnant. The girl admitted consenting to sex (although she was under the influence of alcohol, bought by her boyfriend) but she was below the age of consent. Her parents reported the boy to the police following the pregnancy test.

Scenario E: A 57-year-old man has been found guilty of murder, after he stabbed a 20-year-old man to death with a kitchen knife. The 20-year-old was an intruder, who was in the middle of burgling and vandalising the 57-year-old's house. However, the intruder was walking away from the 57-year-old, towards the exit, at the time of the stabbing.

The scenarios are deliberately designed to lead to some heated debate! Argue your case strongly, but do take note of the alternative views held by your classmates as you should demonstrate your awareness of a range of views.

In fact, if you were a judge or a magistrate, you would have less leeway than you just had in that activity. Some crimes carry a mandatory prison sentence, for example. However, there would be occasions when you could choose between a prison sentence or a non-custodial sentence (for example), the length of a prison sentence and the size of a fine. Those questions about the *purposes of punishment* would all factor into those decisions. But there would be other factors too: aggravating factors (those that would make a judge or magistrate choose a harsher sentence) or mitigating factors (those that would lead them to a more lenient sentence.

Let's add a couple of extra factors to the scenarios above. The woman in Scenario A was a professional, a lawyer of previously good character. The pop-singer in Scenario B was suffering from depression and had been referred to a therapist by their GP only a month earlier. The girl in Scenario C has a six-month-old daughter. The 17-year-old in Scenario D is the only carer of his disabled mother. The 57-year-old in Scenario E is a government minister.

Would you take any of these factors into account when sentencing? How might they impact on your original decisions? Argue again!!

Search some newspaper websites online (both local and national websites) in search of a handful of real sentencing decisions. Try and understand the reason behind the sentence in each case. If you go to http://ybtj.justice.gov.uk/ you can try out some more sentences in the "you be the judge" game.

F. Miscarriages of Justice

Go to http://www.innocent.org.uk to find examples of people who have been or still are in prison who protest their innocence and who campaigners think have been wrongly convicted. Using this website research several case studies and share these with your classmates. You should consider:

- What was the evidence in the original trial?
- Why were they originally convicted?
- What was wrong with the original conviction?
- What process has been followed since then? Have there been any appeals? What did the judge say at any appeal?

Famous case studies you could use include cases like the Guildford Four and the Birmingham Six. In both cases, the IRA set off bombs in pubs in England and people were put in prison for the offences who were later released on appeal after their initial convictions were quoshed. In the case of the Guildford Four, the original judge said that he wished they had been convicted of high treason so that he could have issued a death sentence.

Test Yourself:
1. What is an indictable offence?
2. What is an either-way offence?
3. Where are the initial hearings of all criminal cases?
4. How many people sit on a jury?
5. Give an example of a miscarriage of justice

CRIME JUSTICE AND PUNISHMENT EXAM-STYLE QUESTIONS

Questions are always grouped in pairs, one 15 mark question and the other a 25 mark question. Both should be properly written and well-structured essays. A lot of the marks available are for the argument and the analysis, the communication and your ability to synthesize material from across the whole A Level. There are relatively few marks available for what you know (knowledge and understanding) compared with otherA Levels, but of course you can't analyse, synthesize and communicate fresh air! You do need some appropriate and relevant content to work your magic on!

Here are a few questions to try. Initially just jot down everything you might want to bring into the question, then try and put it together as an argument.

01 Explain and comment on the jury system in criminal trials (15 marks)

02 "There is no such thing as a typical criminal". Critically evaluate this view (25 marks)

OR

03 Examine the role of the Crown Prosecution Service (CPS) (15 marks)

04 "The main aim of sentencing is rehabilitation". Critically evaluate this view (25 marks)

OR

05 Examine the nature of a criminal trial in the Crown Court (15 marks)

06 Assess the view that crime is always wrong (25 marks)

INTRODUCTION TO POLITICS, POWER AND PARTICIPATION

In AS Citizenship, in Unit 2, you had a clear and broad introduction to UK Government and Politics – particularly in terms of the role of the individual citizen in the political process, but also looking at the nature of power, the relationship between different levels of government, the role of political parties and the impact of the European Union. In this section, you will approach these issues in much more detail and look at some of the bigger issues of the UK political system, as well as its place in the world.

REPRESENTATIVE DEMOCRACY

A. Indirect and direct democracy

Two key terms to understand are *direct* and *indirect democracy*. Of course, democracy literally means "rule by the people". The term "Athenian democracy" is often used to refer to the original ancient Greek version of democracy; the idea that the people literally would take all the decisions by a majority vote. This would be a form of *direct democracy* but, of course, is rather impractical for modern nations with their large and diverse populations. We do still have some examples of *direct democracy* – notably REFERENDUMS – and some countries use many more of these than the UK does. For example, the Republic of Ireland has referendums for all changes to their constitution.

A referendum is a popular vote on a specific issue. The two national referendums that there have been in the UK were in 1975 – over whether to remain in the European Union – and in 2011 over whether to change our voting system to Alternative Vote (more on this later!). There have also been several referendums in specific parts of the UK, e.g. on devolution to Scotland, Wales and Northern Ireland and whether to introduce elected mayors in local government in some English cities.

However, most of our democracy is *indirect democracy*: representative democracy. Rather than making all the decisions ourselves, we elect representatives to take those decisions on our behalf. For example, in General Elections, we vote for Members of Parliament (MPs) who sit in the House of Commons and vote on new legislation. Rather than consult us on every issue, they take the decisions and we decide every five years whether we are happy with how they have represented us.

There are different views about the role of a representative. The English Tory MP and philosopher, Edmund Burke, pointed out that representatives were *not* delegates. It was not the job of an MP to take instruction from their constituents and do what they were told. It was their job to use their judgment, their experience and their knowledge to take what they believed to be the correct decisions. When the next election came along, should the public have been unhappy with their representative's performance, they could choose another.

MPs today have a number of pressures that might influence their decisions and it is sometimes suggested that the democratic pressure from their constituents is not as strong a pressure as it ought to be. As well as being constituency representatives, the vast majority of MPs are also representatives of a political party and may feel stronger bonds of loyalty to the "party line" than to the wishes of their constituents. After all, many people do not know who their MP is and, when they vote in a general election, vote for the party in a general sense rather than for their local representative.

Before moving on, you should ensure that you have:

- Definitions of both direct and indirect democracy
- Examples of both direct and indirect democracy

B. Elections in the UK

The best-known elections in the UK are the General Elections. These take place at least every five years and are where MPs are elected.

Perhaps the most broadly misunderstood element of these elections is quite how they translate into who forms a government and who becomes Prime Minister. Hopefully you were happy with this by the end of AS, but just in case...

The UK Prime Minister is *not* directly elected – they are not like a President. The Prime Minister will (almost) always be the leader of the party with the most seats in Parliament following the General Election. This is why Prime Ministers can come and go without a General Election (e.g. Gordon Brown replacing Tony Blair and John Major replacing Margaret Thatcher). All people are doing in a General Election is voting for their local MP. If any one party has a majority of MPs (which they usually do, thanks to our voting system) then that party forms a government and their leader becomes Prime Minister (formally at the invitation of the Queen but, again, this is just a ceremonial formality).

But there are lots of other elections in the UK too.

- Local elections: we vote for members of County, District and Parish councils (or City Councils)

- European elections: we vote for Members of the European Parliament (MEPs)

- Mayoral elections: in some cities, like London, we vote for the mayor

- Devolved assembly elections: in Scotland, Wales, Northern Ireland and London we vote for members of devolved assemblies (and the Scottish Parliament)

- Police commissioners: since 2012, we vote for police commissioners

- Referendums: we sometimes vote "yes" or "no" to specific questions. The natonal ones we have had in the UK were on whether to stay in the European Union in 1975, and whether to change our voting system to AV in 2011. There have been many local and regional referendums.

In these elections, we do not always use the same voting system, as outlined in the next section.

C. UK electoral systems

In the UK, we have elections using the following systems:

- First past the post (or simple plurality)
- Party List
- Additional Member System
- Single Transferable Vote
- Supplementary Vote

And we had a referendum in 2011 about the possibility of using Alternative Vote for General Elections.

In many ways, the UK is a laboratory experiment of different voting systems! You need to know where these systems are used and have a broad understanding of the advantages and disadvantages of each system.

First Past The Post (Simple Plurality)

This is our system for General Elections and most council elections. It is based on a very simple premise: whichever candidate gets the most votes, wins – regardless of what proportion of the vote they receive.

Actually casting your vote in a First Past the Post election is very straightforward. You simply put a cross next to your preferred candidate.

Counting the votes is also very straightforward: the candidate with the most votes is elected.

So why is the system so controversial? Let us look at it in terms of you, as an individual voter, playing your part in electing the next government of the UK.

Although the election campaign is very much focused on the national picture and which party will form the next government, your vote at a general election is simply for your local MP. If you live in what is known as a "marginal" constituency, this vote can be crucial to the final result. These are constituencies where more than one candidate has a realistic chance of success. For the rest of us, who live in "safe seats" our vote is much less likely to be crucial. If we support our local MP (or his/her party) then we are likely to be pleased with our local result (although we are unlikely to have played a significant part in achieving it). If we support a different candidate, or prefer a different party, then we are likely to be disappointed. And at that point, our vote has done its job. It was counted, but our preferred candidate was unsuccessful. Even if our candidate only got one vote less than the winner, that's it: the winner takes all. Even if more people in the constituency voted for other candidates (put together) than voted for the winner: the winner takes all. So, importantly, the winner does not need 50% of the votes. The winner just needs more votes than the person who came second.

So – one clear disadvantage then: **MPs who are elected to represent the whole constituency might have only received the votes of a minority of their constituents**.

Also – **there are wasted votes**. The wasted votes are those cast for the losing parties but also those **surplus votes** cast for the winner.

But what happens next? As we know, the party with the most MPs almost always gets to form the government, especially if they have the *majority* of seats in Parliament. Under the First Past the Post system, it is normal for one party to get a majority of seats and form a single-party government. The Conservative/Liberal Democrat coalition, elected in 2010, was something of a rarity.

However, it is hardly ever the case that one party will get a majority of the *votes* cast in a general election. The First Past the Post system *over-represents* the winners. Parties getting around 40% of the votes can end up with well over 50% of the seats.

But perhaps the most apparently unfair aspect of the system comes at the other end of the scale. Parties getting perhaps 20 or 30% of the votes cast can get a negligible share of the seats and some parties with a reasonable degree of public support can end up with no seats at all. Why? To get a seat you have to come in first place *somewhere*. If you came in second place *everywhere* you would have no seats. And coming in second place *everywhere* could mean that you got more votes than the party who won the election, as they only have to come in first place in *most* places!

Okay, that rather extreme scenario never happens. But a party like the Liberal Democrats always do far worse in terms of seats than they do in terms of votes, as they do come second in a lot of places. If you want to be successful as a small party it is much better to have localised support (like the Scottish National Party or Plaid Cymru) than to be reasonably popular across the whole country.

So some more disadvantages then:

A winner's bonus (the winner of the election always gets a higher percentage of seats than votes)
Under-representation of third and minority parties

It is even possible for a party to get a majority of seats, and therefore form a single-party government, while actually having *lost* the election in terms of votes. For example, in 1951 Labour got the most votes. In fact they got more votes than they received in any other election before or since. But the Conservatives won the election and had a majority.

HOW? Good question. Labour's vote was overwhelming but geographically concentrated. They did extremely well in their "heartlands" in the industrial north, but the Conservative Party's vote was more widespread, therefore they were able to win more seats. Another contributory factor was the fact that most people in that election voted for one of the two main parties.

So a final disadvantage: **the winning party need not have got the most votes**

That sounds pretty damning, but there are plenty of *advantages* too.

Advantages of First Past the Post:

- **Simplicity**: voters understand how to vote and how their votes are counted
- **Strong constituency link**: There is a clear link between the MP and their constituency (many "proportional" systems have much larger constituencies with several MPs, or some MPs who do not represent a constituency at all)
- **A clear mandate**: The winning party is elected on a clear manifesto and (assuming they have a majority, which they normally do) has a *mandate* to carry out that programme.
- **Strong majority government**: Normally (not in 2010, of course!) one party gets a clear majority and is able to form a strong, stable government

And a quick summary of those disadvantages:

- **MPs who are elected to represent the whole constituency might have only received the votes of a minority of their constituents.**

- **there are wasted votes**
- **a winner's bonus**
- **under-representation of third and minority parties**
- **the winning party need not have got the most votes**

Party List

There are a few different types of list system. In the UK we use it for European parliamentary elections. This is with a regional closed-list system. This means that people vote for MEPs for a *region* (a large, multi-member constituency) from *closed lists*. In other words, people vote "Labour", "Conservative", "Liberal Democrat", etc rather than for individual candidates. When the votes are counted, the parties are allocated MEPs based on their share of the vote. If the Labour Party is given two MEPs, then the top two people on their list are duly elected.

Some places use an "open" list where voters can write-in specific candidates if they prefer somebody lower down the list. This rarely has much impact on the result, but "seems" more democratic.

There are list systems that are not regional, for example for Israeli general elections there is a national list: all the votes are counted for the whole country and seats handed out proportionately.

The key *advantage* of a Party List system is its *proportionality*. To a large extent, the number of seats held by each party broadly reflects the votes cast.

It is also *relatively* simple. Voters simply put a cross next to their preferred party. How those votes get converted into seats is a little less straightforward than in a First Past the Post election, but certainly simpler than some of the alternatives.

There are disadvantages, though. There is less of a clear MP-constituency link. Most people cannot name one of their MEPs. However, on the flipside, it is more likely that there is one MEP who you feel represents your views reasonably well. If you are a Conservative voter in a safe Labour seat or a Labour voter in a safe Conservative seat it can be a frustrating business. But, as a voter in Yorkshire and the Humber, you have Labour, Conservative, Liberal Democrat, UKIP and BNP MEPs to choose from. Although that does bring me to another *disadvantage*: under this system there is an increased chance of extremist parties like the BNP being elected. Parties can get a seat with relatively low levels of support. In Yorkshire and the Humber for example, BNP MEP Andrew Brons received only 9% of the vote in 2009, but got 20% of the seats (one seat out of five). The Conservative Party, with 25% of the vote (nearly three times as many votes as the BNP) also only got one MEP for the region. Therefore, although the overall result for the country is quite proportional, locally it can be rather disproportionate. This is because of the complex "D'Hondt method" of attributing seats. Don't worry – you don't need to understand the Maths for this! Or for single transferrable vote, which is coming later. But mathematicians among you might want to look into this further.

Advantages:

- **Proportionality** The outcomes of party list elections are much more proportional than First Past the Post elections – i.e. the percentage of seats for each party broadly reflects the percentage of votes they received
- **Voter choice** Voters feel that they have less need to use *tactical* voting, as their first choice party might well get a seat in the multi-member constituencies.
- **Simplicity** Although the way in which votes translate into seats is quite complex, it is very simple for the voter: simply putting a cross next to the preferred party

Disadvantages
- **Less clear constituency-MP link** Because of multi-member constituencies you no longer have one MP but several (counter argument is that you might have voted for one of your MPs!)
- **More chance of extremist parties getting elected**
- **Disproportionate on local scale**
- **Too much power for political parties** Political parties choose the list, so voters just vote "Labour" or "Conservative" rather than for individuals – this takes power away from

individual voters to choose their representative (rather than just their party). An alternative has an "open list" where voters can write in a preferred candidate rather than have to follow the party's list.

Additional Member System

In Scotland and Wales, for the Scottish Parliament and Welsh Assembly, a different system is used. It is the Additional Member System which is also described as a *hybrid* system. It is called a hybrid system because it combines *majoritarian* and *proportional* principles. Effectively, there are two elections. Each voter gets to vote for their local representative and for a party list. The first votes are counted and the local MSPs (Members of the Scottish Parliament) or AMs (Assembly Members) are elected. This is a straightforward first past the post election. (There is an alternative version of this where this part of the process is done using AV – it is called AV+). This has all the advantages and disadvantages previously listed. However, now a number of "top up" members are elected via a party list election. The list votes are used to ensure a more proportional final result with often the second and third placed parties getting a good set of "top up" members. This has tended to prevent there from being majority governments in Scotland and Wales although the SNP did manage to win a majority in Scotland thanks to securing a majority of votes.

In 1997, the new Labour government commissioned the Liberal Democrat peer Roy Jenkins to investigate various electoral systems to decide which was the best. He concluded that AV+ (which is very similar to this process) was the best, but it was never adopted. Supporters of hybrid systems comment that they combine the advantages of both types of electoral system, although critics say they also combine the disadvantages!

Advantages of Additional Member System

Proportional – The party-list part of the process tends to lead to a proportional, or broadly proportional result

Strong constituency link – the First Past the Post element of the process means that each constituency has a clear representative.

Disadvantages of the Additional Member System

Complex – Although both parts are relatively simple for the voter (a cross by a candidate and then a cross by a party) some voters have got confused by the presence of two votes in the same election

Usually creates coalition government – Not necessarily a disadvantage of course! Some people really like coalition government as they feel more than one party should be represented in government. However coalitions tend to be less stable than majority governments and can be criticised for making policy after the election in the form of behind-the-scenes negotiations rather than following a manifesto with a clear mandate

Single Transferrable Vote

Supporters of *proportional representation* mostly favour Single Transferrable Vote (STV), which is the electoral system that is generally regarded to produce the most *proportional* result of all (except, perhaps, for a *national* list system). It is also by far the most complex of the electoral systems and you (fortunately) do not have to understand it in any detail to bring it into an answer about electoral systems in your Citizenship exam!

In this system, the voter ranks the candidates in their order of preference. So, their first choice would be marked "1", second favourite "2" and so on. This part of the process is the same as the much simpler Alternative Vote or AV (see below). What makes STV so complex is not so much what the voter has to do (although that has caused some difficulties in Northern Ireland where this system is used) but how those votes are translated into seats. Like in the Party List system STV requires big multi-member constituencies. As such, the process is not choosing one MP but several, so the ballot paper might include multiple candidates from the same party. Candidates have to reach a certain quota of votes to be elected. Each time the votes are counted the losing candidate is disqualified and their votes transferred to their second preference and so on until all the positions are filled. If you chose unpopular candidates it's quite possible your vote will ultimately help your 5th or 6th favourite candidate get elected! When this system has been used in the UK it has tended to result in a large increase in spoilt ballot papers, simply because of people not understanding what they are meant to do. It is used in Northern Ireland because it virtually guarantees that no one party can win an outright majority and Northern Ireland's troubled past means that broad coalitions are very desirable. However, many people prefer a single-party majority government which STV is very unlikely to ever produce.

Advantages of STV

Proportional STV is the most proportional of the electoral systems used in the UK. As such, it fully represents minor parties and does not give unfair advantages to the bigger parties. (It is perhaps unsurprising that the Liberal Democrats have tended to favour STV for general elections, as studies estimate that it would have greatly improved their results in all general elections and would regularly create the situation where they hold the balance of power in a hung parliament).

Disadvantages of STV

Very complicated
Increased chance of representation for extremist parties
Always creates coalition government

Supplementary Vote

The last system currently used in some UK elections is Supplementary Vote (or SV) which is similar to AV (see below) only it is used for electing one individual to a specific position (e.g. Mayor of London) rather than multiple members of parliament. It is used for elected mayors (e.g. in London). Voters get to choose a first and second preference (they don't have to state a second preference if they don't have one). If nobody gets over 50% of the first preference votes all but the top two candidates are eliminated and the second preferences counted. At this point (unless it is was a dead heat which is extremely unlikely) somebody must get over 50% of the votes and be elected.

Advantages of SV

Reduces tactical voting People can vote for the party/candidate they *really* want even if they haven't got much chance of winning safe in the knowledge that doing so does not benefit the candidate they *don't* want to win – they can give their second preference to the candidate they would prefer out of the front-runners. E.g. a Green Party supporter might have preferred Ken Livingstone to Boris Johnson. Under FPTP they might have felt compelled to vote for Livingstone or to risk splitting the "left-wing" vote and allowing Johnson to win. With SV they could vote Green 1 and Livingstone 2. However, it arguably just leads to a different type of tactical voting with the front-runners "courting" the voters of other parties to try and secure their second preferences.

Forces candidates to go beyond their natural support base Boris Johnson knew that he could not win London Mayor with the votes of Conservative supporters alone; the same with Ken Livingstone and Labour supporters. As such they had to try and appeal to other voters making for a less *tribal* and party-political election (at least in theory!)

At least half the people voted for the winner Of course, they might have preferred a different candidate, but at least half the people who used both their votes gave one of them to the winning candidate.

Disadvantages of SV

No point giving a second preference to a candidate who isn't one of the front runners If your first preference was Green and your second UKIP, then neither of your votes would end up featuring in the final count as both your preferred candidates would have been disqualified at the first stage.

No point having a second preference if your first is one of the front-runners Similarly Ken Livingstone and Boris Johnson supporters did not really have a second vote as their guy was pretty much guaranteed a place in the run-off at the end.

Still a "winner takes all" system In terms of proportionality, it really doesn't matter how many votes the losing candidates get.

Alternative Vote

Alternative Vote (AV) is not used in any UK elections at present but, in 2011, there was a referendum to consider changing to this system for UK general elections. The "yes" campaign was led by the Liberal Democrats and some Labour MPs. However, AV is an odd system in that not many people are very excited about it. Nick Clegg – the figurehead of the "yes" campaign for AV once described it as a "miserable little compromise". Although not used in any public elections in the UK, it is used in some organisations; for example the Labour Party uses AV to elect the Party Leader and Deputy Leader.

AV is a "majoritarian" system: it still produces one MP for each constituency and is just as likely to result in majority governments as First Past the Post. The main way it differs from First Past the Post is that the successful MPs have received the support of 50% of the electorate. Like with STV and SV, voters rank the candidates in order of preference. If any candidate gets 50% of first preferences they are automatically elected (as such, many "safe seats" would not be affected in any way). If no candidates receive 50% there follows a series of disqualifications and redistributions until a candidate can claim the magic 50% and take the seat. In more marginal seats, it is possible that this redistribution of second, third and fourth preferences *could* lead to a change in the result. Winston Churchill argued that the system meant some elections could be determined by "the most worthless votes of the most worthless candidates" as the second preferences of the least popular candidates could determine the outcome.

Advantages:

Reduces tactical voting: Voters do not need to choose the "lesser evil" but give their first preference to their favourite candidate or party without worrying about "splitting the vote". However, it might just move the tactical vote to the second preference.

Arguably reduces tribalism and encourages pluralism: In many constituencies, parties would not be able to rely simply on their core voters but would need to make links with those with different viewpoints.

Disadvantages:

Still disproportionate: A change to AV would not deal with the main concern people have about First Past the Post

Increased power and role of least popular candidates: Winston Churchill's point from above.

So – what do you think?

Should we change our voting system or keep it the same? Consider having a debate in your class in the subject and be prepared to defend your view.

C. Our representatives

Who are our representatives? Make a list of all your political representatives. (Unless you're very politically engaged you will probably have to do an internet search for some of them). Find out:

Your MP
Your MEPs. Because the European Parliament uses the Party List voting system, you will have several MEPs from several political parties, not just one.
Your local councillors. Depending where you live you might have several councillors operating at different levels. Many of us have parish (or town) councillors, district councillors and county councillors, while in other areas the district and county councils are brought together as a "unitary" or metropolitan council.

If you live in London, Scotland, Wales or Northern Ireland you will also have other representatives in your devolved assembly or parliament.

Have you met or otherwise engaged with any of these people? How well do you feel they represent your views? Have they ever sought your opinion on anything? How would you contact them, if you wanted them to raise an issue on your behalf?

Now you have identified your representatives: what are they like? How old are they? Are they men or women? What is their ethnicity? Can you discover anything about their social class or professional background? Although you are likely to have identified a range of people, the predominant group is (as with judges in an earlier section) white, middle-aged (or older), middle-class (or richer) men. 62% of MPs are white men aged over 40.

There are now more women MPs then there ever have been at 142 (as of the 2010 Parliament); that is 22% of the House. Although this makes the House of Commons more representative than the judiciary, it still shows that women are hugely under-represented in politics. There are only 26 minority ethnic MPs, accounting for 4% of the MPs, compared with approximately 12% of the general population. Perhaps the most dramatic differences between parliament and people are in terms of social class, as difficult as that is to measure. People often use education to give some indication of this. 90% of MPs are university graduates, compared with 20% of the adult population. More than a quarter of MPs went to Oxford or Cambridge. Over a third of the current MPs attended a fee-paying school (compared with less than 10% of the general population) and there are 20 MPs who attended the same school (Eton) - nearly as many as the total number of minority ethnic MPs.

The inevitable question relating to this is: does it matter? One MP can't possibly be socially representative of all their constituents. All constituencies will have a range of ages, ethnicities, social class and both genders. A man has to be able to represent a woman in parliament and vice versa. However, many would argue that when a certain section of society is so dominant in Parliament (ie rich white men) this *must* impact on how well women, minority ethnic groups, the poor and young people are represented. Individual rich white men may well do an excellent job of representing the poor black women in their constituency. The question is more whether the culture of parliament (and other representative bodies) is rooted in what is actually quite a small section of society. Middle-class problems seem more real and urgent, the poor are "other". There is general policy and then there are special areas of policy for dealing with "minority" problems, "women's issues" and "social exclusion". Arguably, everybody except rich white men are treated as "special interest groups".

People who argue that a certain section of society is dominant are sometimes described as *radical elitists* (they are termed *radical* elitists to distinguish them from *classical* elitists who believed that a certain section of society *should* be dominant!) Radical elitists and Marxists might point to the fact that the vast majority of people are employees not employers, and yet politicians spend much more of their time serving the interests of the latter rather than the former. This, they would argue, is because that is the class or social group they come from and that has a greater influence on them than democratic pressure from their constituents. Critics would point to laws like the minimum wage to show that this is not always the case. They would also point out that the professional background of MPs is much more likely to be in law or education than in industry.

D. Citizen participation

How do individual citizens participate in terms of *being represented*?

First we elected our representatives. We elect MPs at general elections, MEPs at European elections, councillors at a range of local elections.

However, most people do not vote in European or local elections, meaning even that most basic form of active citizenship is a minority pursuit.

Far fewer citizens are involved *before* the elections, either in terms of helping select candidates, being a candidate or being involved in election campaigns. Anybody can join a political party and, in most parties, party members are involved in selecting local candidates for elections. The candidates, too, are party members. For general elections and European elections the winners become professional politicians, but victorious council candidates are unpaid volunteers who fit their work as a representative around their job (unless they are retired, which a disproportionately high number of them are). Party members also help candidates with their election campaigns, distributing leaflets, *canvassing*, displaying posters, etc.

What about after the elections? The essence of a representative democracy is that we elect representatives and, if we do not like what they do on our behalf, we vote them out at the next election. But between elections, representatives need to know what their constituents want from them, and they also engage in a range of *casework* on behalf of constituents who approach them with concerns.

People are likely to contact their local council if they are concerned about issues impacting on their local area or neighbourhood, for example:

- Noisy neighbours
- Fly-tipping
- Planning concerns (e.g. somebody has built a new extention and you don't think they had planning permission)
- Concerns relating to council services (such as bin collection)

People are likely to contact their MP over concerns over issues of national importance, issues with a direct link to national government, or over local issues where they do not feel that their councillor has dealt with the matter satisfactorily, for example:

- Experiences relating to public services, e.g. NHS, policing and crime, benefits
- Concerns relating to current proposed legislation (e.g. opposition to a particular bill)

Individual citizens are actually quite unlikely to contact their MEPs and this is perhaps one reason why they seem rather remote and less accountable than their Westminster and City Hall colleagues.

Citizens might also contact representatives as part of a group. Pressure groups, of various sorts (see AS modules) will access representatives via *lobbying*, petitions, coordinated letter-writing, etc.

How else do citizens get their views across to their representatives?

An increasingly popular option is to sign an e-petition on the government's website. Given sufficient signatures (100,000 plus) the issue will be considered for debate in the House of Commons by the Backbench Business Committee. Since this initiative was introduced in 2011 there have been 20 debates[1] (compared with many, many hundreds of popular petitions). To be debated, the petition must receive the backing of (at least) one backbench MP and the committee must consider it sufficiently topical and sufficiently distinct from other recent parliamentary debates to be worthy of discussion. The Backbench Business Committee is not allocated a lot of time each week for debates as most of the House's business is made-up of government legislation. Petitions from the public are only one of the sources of topics they may wish to debate in this limited time.

Test Yourself:

1. What does PR stand for?
2. What is meant by the term coalition government?
3. Why do people say there are *wasted votes* in First Past the Post elections? Explain *two* ways votes can be wasted.
4. Which elections in the UK use a closed regional Party List system?
5. What was unusual about the results of UK general elections in 1951 and 1974?

---

[1] This number is, of course, subject to change. The point is that most petitions do not actually get debated in Parliament and are even less likely to lead to an actual change in the law

PARLIAMENT & GOVERNMENT

A. UK political parties & ideology

The three main parties in Britain are: The Conservative Party, The Labour Party and the Liberal Democrat Party. In some parts of the United Kingdom there are other large parties (such as the SNP in Scotland, Plaid Cymru in Wales and the Democratic Unionsist Party, Sinn Fein, the Ulster Unionist Party and the SDLP in Northern Ireland). For the purposes of this chapter we will be focusing on those first three main parties, but don't forget about the others altogether!

What are political parties for?
They have a number of key roles:
- Organising the vote – without the important work of political parties it is very likely that election turnout (the percentage of registered voters who actually cast a vote) would be much lower than it is. Party volunteers post out leaflets, do canvassing, organise TV and radio broadcasts and other forms of advertising. They even give supporters lifts to the polling station! Often it is only through the work of a political party that many electors even know that an election is happening!
- Representing the interests of their members
- Forming a government or providing an alternative "government-in-waiting"
- Holding the government to account (in the case of opposition parties)

The Conservative Party

The Conservative Party developed from the old Tory Party, which was the party of the aristocracy and landed gentry. Traditional Tories had a strong belief in traditions and maintaining the old order. They were strongly opposed to the "foreign" influence of liberalism. They argued that the United Kingdom had *"ancient liberties"* and that its people were truly free, while the people of France and the USA and other places experiencing liberal revolutions would in fact be the victims of tyranny. For these conservatives, rapid change was always bad; social change is best when it is evolutionary and gradual.

Through the 19th century the position of the Conservatives changed somewhat. At times they were the "one nation" party – determined to keep the country together and prevent class war, which included supporting policies to help the poor as well as focusing on patriotism and national pride. At other times they took over from the old Liberal party as being the party of *laissez-faire*, that is the party that saw a minimal role for government and preferred to leave things to the free market.

In the late 20th century this became the dominant ideological position of the Conservative Party, associated with Margaret Thatcher and what is known as "New Right" politics. The New Right was a mixture of *neo-liberalism* (the *laisser-faire* economics previously mentioned) and *neo-conservatism* (a strong belief in traditional values and tough policies on law and order and defence).

This position, coupled with a scepticism about the European Union, still seems to be a dominant ideological view within the Conservative Party today. However some conservatives were worried that this position led to them being seen as "the nasty party". When David Cameron became leader of the Conservative Party he put a lot of effort into changing the *image* of the party, and this included some changes to ideology as well.

The key things David Cameron did to change the Conservative Party's image were to express total support for the NHS and to focus on environmental (or "green") issues. This latter move also led to a change in the party's official logo, from a blue torch to a green tree.

Go to the Conservative Party's official website and find some of their current policies. How do these policies fit into the ideologies described above? Is the party still committed to the environment and protecting the NHS?

The Labour Party

In the late 19th century there was a growth in trade unionism in the UK (small workers' "guilds" merged together to form big general unions). At the same time there were a few small socialist and radical liberal parties who proposed policies that were likely to most appeal to the working class, a group who were just starting to be allowed to vote for the first time. In 1900, some of these political groups got together with the big unions and formed the Labour Representation Committee which, in 1906, became the Labour Party. Although there have been big changes over the years, this mixture of trade union and political roots as well as radical, even revolutionary, socialist ideas along with moderate and reformist ones has always characterised the party. At various times it has led to disagreements and even splits. For most of its history, the moderate, reformist wing of the party has been "in charge".

The Conservatives were in power from 1979 to 1997 and, by the late 1980s, Labour supporters were beginning to fear that British society had changed in such a way that Labour could no longer win an election on the sort of programme and policy platform that had been successful for them in the past. They felt that changes in society, some of them implemented by Conservative PM Margaret Thatcher, meant that appealing primarily to working-class voters could not win an election. A group of Labour thinkers began to think that Labour needed a serious change of image, but also a change of policy, to appeal to a generation who, rather than considering inequality to be fundamentally unfair, considered inequality to be natural and normal and admired individuals who made lots of money.

This was eventually to become *New Labour*. It did not reject everything Labour had previously stood for. It was very much rooted in the reformist, moderate tradition of the party. It continued to champion the NHS and funding for schools and it argued for a minimum wage (something that had been Labour policy since the party was founded but no "old Labour" government had been able to implement). At the same time, it began to distance itself from the trade unions (offering them "fairness not favours"), embrace many of the free market ideas of the Thatcher years and abandon policies for renationalising public utilities. It was enthusiastically pro-European ("old Labour" was much more sceptical) and abandoned its past opposition to nuclear weapons.

Many would argue that the change was successful: Labour won the 1997 general election with a landslide and went on to do even better in the 2001 election. However, by 2010, many in the Labour Party questioned whether Tony Blair, Peter Mandelson and Gordon Brown had gone too far in supporting big business and the free market; Britain's role in the Iraq War had led to some of the deepest divisions in Labour's history. Ed Miliband declared, on becoming leader, that "New Labour is dead".

Why not do some research on what you think has replaced it? There is a range of views on this. Find out what is meant by "Blue Labour", "the Purple Book", "Red Labour" and "In the Black Labour".

The Liberal Democrat Party

The Liberal Democrat Party is a much younger party than the other two. It was formed in the 1980s out of the merging of the Liberal Party and the SDP (Social Democratic Party). The Liberal Party was an old party that emerged from the Whigs and for many years was the only political rival to the Conservative Party (or Tories).

For much of the 19th century it was associated with free market economics and a "small state". The main principles of liberalism are freedom and rights, but for early liberals, freedom *from the government* was the key issue. In the late 19th and early 20th centuries, some liberals began to argue that freedom from the government was of no great use if you could not exercise that freedom. In other words, governments perhaps had a role after all, in empowering people. As such, the 1906 Liberal government introduced state pensions and free school meals and slowly began the foundations of the welfare state that would be built upon by post-war Labour and

Conservative governments. Indeed, the intellectual founder of the British welfare state, William Beveridge, was a Liberal.

However, that "positive liberal" government was to be the last. Britain's political system tends to support a two-party system and, as the Labour Party grew, it turned into the main alternative to the Conservative Party and the Liberals became smaller and smaller.

They got a new lease of life in the 1980s in the form a new ally. After the 1979 election, the Labour Party briefly turned left and brought in quite radical policies on leaving the European Union and NATO, nationalising successful British companies and unilaterally getting rid of nuclear weapons. A section of the "moderate wing" of the Labour Party broke away and formed the SDP. They contested the 1983 and 1987 elections as the SDP-Liberal Alliance where these two "centre" parties agreed not to stand candidates against each other. After 87 they chose to become one party, the Liberal Democrats.

They came together around policies such as enthusiastic support for the European Union and for electoral reform (wanting to change First Past the Post for Single Transferable Vote).

"Positive liberalism" and social democracy are not greatly dissimilar ideologies and the two parties merged happily. However, in the last few years, some of the Liberal Democrat liberals have been seeking to revisit their classical liberal (laissez faire) past and have talked about Orange Book Liberalism. These liberals, like Nick Clegg, Danny Alexander and David Laws, have found the coalition with the Conservative Party since 2010 a more comfortable experience than some of the social democrats, like Vince Cable and Simon Hughes.

What will happen to the Liberal Democrats after the next election?

There is an argument to suggest that the three main parties are now grouped around the "centre" of British politics with few big ideological differences between them. They are all essentially "liberal" parties who believe largely in the private sector and free-market capitalism alongside a welfare state and free healthcare. They are all "pro-business" and while there might be differences on the level of their enthusiasm for the European Union or what level they would like the minimum wage to be set at, these are differences of *policy* rather than differences of ideology or principle.

Others would argue that there are still fundamental differences between the parties. They would point to the different responses to the economic crisis from 2008 when the Labour government used the state to bail out banks and pump money into the economy while the Conservative Party urged austerity and public sector cuts. However, both parties have been in power at different phases of the crisis and whether they would have behaved very differently from each other in the same situation is something of a debatable point.

B. Powers of Parliament

Parliament is described as *bicameral* in that it has *two chambers*: The House of Commons and the House of Lords. (The House of Lords is currently in the middle of attempts to reform it and so could, theoretically, change significantly from how it is described in this book in a relatively short space of time).

Parliament has four key roles:

Representation
Legislation
Scrutiny
Accountability

Parliament's representative role is primarily carried out by the House of Commons, as described in the previous chapter.

The *legislative* role of parliament is carried out by both houses.

Legislation refers to *laws*. While laws are still working their way through Parliament they are called *bills*, once they have been given Royal Assent by the monarch, they are called *acts*. For example the Human Rights Act (1998) was the Human Rights Bill until it had passed successfully through both chambers and had been signed by the Queen (the Royal Assent). This final stage of a bill is a formality: the Queen does not refuse to sign any bills.

You considered the passage of legislation in AS Citizenship. At A2 you are rewarded for synopticity/synthesis; revise your AS work on the legislative process now.

Parliament's *scrutiny* role mostly happens in committees. Select Committees in the Commons and the Lords scrutinise the work of the government in a range of policy areas. For example, the Home Affairs Select Committee scrutinises the work of the home office in considerable detail and can request the presence of ministers, civil servants and expert witnesses as well as asking for papers. It does not have the legal powers of summons that a court has, but it would be unwise to refuse to appear at a select committee or to withold documents from them. Other parliamentary committees are established specifically to consider the details of new legislation as it passes throught the "committee stage". This is part of Parliament's legislative function, but it subjects proposed legislation to detailed scrutiny. In the House of Lords the committee stage is carried out by the whole house rather than in small committees.

Select Committees are also one of the more effective ways in which parliament can hold the government of the day *to account*. The other famous way in which parliament carries out its *accountability* role is through Prime Minister's and Ministers' questions. Members can ask oral or written questions and will get answers. If a member primarily wants information then a written question is likely to be more effective as it will elicit a written, detailed response. Oral questions are used more to try and catch the Prime Minister or Secretary of State off their guard, to embarrass them or bring an issue into public attention. Prime Minister's Questions in particular receive a large amount of media interest, especially the exchange between the Prime Minister and the Leader of the Opposition.

However, some would argue that parliamentary questions are not very effective at holding the government to account. If we take Prime Minister's questions as an example, most members can only ask one question and have no opportunity to come back even if the PM avoids answering the question altogether. It is much more an opportunity for getting on the television and delivering memorable lines than for actually holding the government accountable for its actions. Some would argue that Select Committees are more effective at this, but you could question their success too. The government does not have to act on the recommendations of committees and the committees have to try and reach a consensus meaning that while their conclusions are usually thorough they are only rarely contentious.

C. Powers of the Prime Minister

The theoretical powers of a Prime Minister are quite considerable although they have, arguably, been reduced in recent years. However, different Prime Ministers appear to have more or less powers depending on several factors, including: the size of their government's majority in Parliament, their popularity and their style and personality.

The roles of a UK Prime Minister:

Head of government
*Although the UK PM is **not** the Head of State (that is the monarch) s/he is the head of government, the chief of the executive.*

Chair of Cabinet
This involves setting the agenda for Cabinet meetings and chairing the actual proceedings. In case you have forgotten, the Cabinet is the committee of senior ministers who, theoretically at least, run the country – made up of all the heads of government departments.

Chief Appointing Officer
The UK PM's powers of patronage (i.e. giving people jobs) used to be much broader than they are today. Many official appointments are now officially carried out by an independent appointments commission. So the PM no longer personally appoints members of the House of Lords, judges, bishops,

senior civil servants, heads of the armed forces, etc. However s/he does appoint the members of the Cabinet and other government positions.

Chief spokesperson overseas
Although the Cabinet does have a Foreign Secretary (head of the Foreign and Commonwealth Office) the PM is the key figure when it comes to speaking for the UK overseas. At international summits or receiving foreign heads of state, it is the PM who represents the UK (rather than the Foreign Secretary, or the Queen – other than at purely formal or ceremonial occasions)

Chief spokesperson for the government
It is also the PM's duty to answer for the government, both to Parliament and to the Press. Of course other members of the government do this, and the PM's press appearances are rather rare, but ultimately the PM is responsible

Leader of governing party
It is also the case that the PM is the leader of the party of government. It is theoretically possible that a PM might not be the national leader of a party (e.g. if Ed Miliband lost his parliamentary seat at a General Election but the Labour Party won a majority, he would not be automatically removed as party leader) however, s/he would always be the leader of the party in Parliament

The powers of a UK Prime Minister:

The actual *powers* of a Prime Minister are less clear. They can appoint, move and sack ministers. Many of their other roles are carried out in concert with their Cabinet and much will depend on their Prime Ministerial style whether they take a *presidential* approach or a more *collegiate* and *consensual* approach.

The so-called "Royal Prerogatives" (powers that are theoretically in the hands of the Queen) also belong to the Prime Minister, e.g. signing treaties (this can be very important – all EU legislation enters UK law via treaties) and declaring war. Gordon Brown, as Prime Minister, anounced that he wanted to hand that particular prerogative to Parliament, although a specific legislative attempt to do that was dropped in 2010.

Traditionally, an important power of the Prime Minister has been to set the date of the next election (within the five years maximum term). However, David Cameron has abandoned that power, introducing *fixed-term* parliaments for the first time in the UK. As such, we know exactly when the next General Election will be (barring extraordinary and unlikely circumstances). This was often viewed as quite an important power for a Prime Minister as s/he could time the election at his/her best advantage and at the least convenient time for the Opposition. For that reason it has been quite rare for five full years to pass between elections. It is yet to be seen whether this is a temporary change for this coalition government, or a more long-term change.

There are two models of *executive power* in the UK: *prime ministerial government* and *cabinet government*. The idea of cabinet government is the traditional UK approach whereby the prime minister is just *primus inter pares* ("first among equals") and runs the country with the other Cabinet ministers: government by committee. A prime minister who takes this approach will be *collegiate*, will let colleagues use their initiative and will not try and stamp his/her authority on all decisions and all areas of government. Arguably most prime ministers prior to Margaret Thatcher followed this approach (although the theory of prime ministerial government originated during the premierships of Harold Wilson and James Callaghan in the 1960s and 1970s). Prime ministerial government refers to a situation where the Prime Minister completely dominates the executive. In these situations, the Cabinet is little more than a rubber stamp for decisions taken elsewhere. Margaret Thatcher and Tony Blair are often cited as the best examples of this style of prime minister. When David Cameron was elected he said that he wanted to bring back Cabinet government. To a certain extent he would appear to have done so (although he is unable to dominate Cabinet in the same way as some of his predecessors because of the practicalities of coalition government rather than because of his style, approach or theory). However, the media is often critical of more collegiate leaders (John Major was always portrayed as weak, for example) and prefers strong leaders. However, when things start to go wrong, a prime ministerial (or "presidential") leader will tend to get the lion's share of the blame. It is for that reason that Margaret Thatcher was personally associated with the poll tax (for example) much more than the responsible ministers, and the same with Tony Blair and the Iraq War.

BRITAIN IN THE WORLD

A. Britain in the European Union

The European Union, like many other international political bodies, has its roots in the end of the Second World War. Many European politicians were horrified that, so soon after the First World War, the continent of Europe had once again been torn apart by conflict. People from a range of different political perspectives agreed that the future of Europe had to lie in cooperation rather than confrontation. A leading advocate of the concept of European union was Winston Churchill, who argued for a United States of Europe (although it is questionable whether he ever imagined that Britain might be a part of such a state). The early case for some form of European union had many causes including conflict prevention, but also anti-communism (many saw a united western Europe as a powerful bulwark against an expansionist Soviet Union) and economic change (many saw a Europe that worked together as a single common market as a potential competitor to an apparently all-powerful United States of America.) As such, early support for European union was broad, as it had an appeal to peaceful romantics, internationalists, hawkish red-baiters and Europe's capitalists all at the same time. In the early stages of the union, the economic agenda was to the fore, but there was always a long-term political strategy towards greater political union too, with very early EEC documents referring to the desirability of a currency union and of *supranational* political institutions.

Public opinion has always been split in the UK about membership of pan-European bodies and, as such, the UK was late to the party, not joining the EEC until 1970 by which time it was very much an established body with existing rules, institutions and aims. Within five years, the British people were voting in a referendum – the first and (so far, at the time of writing) only UK referendum on EU membership. The people voted convincingly to remain within the EU. This was perhaps unsurprising as the leaderships of all main parties and most of the media was solidly behind staying in. Only the left wing of the Labour Party and the furthest right fringes of the Conservative Party argued for a "No" vote in 1975. It was presented as an extreme position in the media at the time, although it is arguable that it is now the mainstream position in the UK.

Those who voted "Yes" in 1975 but are sceptical of the EU now (like UKIP leader Nigel Farage) argue that the thing has changed beyond all recognition. They say that in 1975 they voted to remain in an economic free-trade area – a common market – not to join a political entity that (from their perspective) was becoming ever more like the United States of Europe that

Winston Churchill described. Those who argued for a "No" vote in 1975 retort that the future of the EU was already mapped out in 1975, and the aspirations for a single currency (what was to become the Euro) and greater political union were already present in the treaties of the community, had people only listened to the "No" campaigners at the time.

Whatever the truth of that, support for a eurosceptic position certainly appears to have grown in recent years, with the right-wing eurosceptic party UKIP reaping the rewards in terms of votes, especially in European elections. However, the Conservative Party fought the 2001 General Election campaign, when William Hague was leader, predominantly on a eurosceptic ticket, with the main election slogan being "Keep the Pound" and yet had one of their worst election performances in 100 years. As such, while a eurosceptic position appears to be popular, it does not appear to be a fundamental position when it comes to influencing voters in a General Election.

Furthermore, the Europe debate has become entwined with an immigration debate and many of UKIP's voters are primarily concerned about the issue of unrestricted migration within the EU rather than other aspects of the union. Of course, UK citizens also benefit from freedom of movement with many thousands choosing to live and work in France, Spain and on meditarranean islands. Furthermore, the examples of European countries that have prospered outside the EU that eurosceptics often provide (Norway and Switzerland – both very prosperous, European, non-EU nations) are (unlike the UK) members of the Schengen Agreement which means they have open borders with the rest of the Schengen area (most of the EU). This means that, apart from anything else, students in other parts of Europe can benefit from Norway's excellent, free university education!

How does the EU work?

The legislative process and general working of the EU is quite a complex one. This complexity of institutions is probably the reason why many in the UK consider the EU to be overly bureaucratic. In fact the EU is not an enormous bureaucracy – it has a similar number of officials as a large city council in Britain, such as Leeds. But it does have a rather opaque decision-making system that certainly seems to lack democratic legitimacy.

The broad agenda is set by the heads of state/heads of government in the *Council of the European Union* – a regular summit meeting. All EU legislation begins life in the *European Commission* – the bureaucracy in Brussels, made up of commissioners appointed by the governments of each EU member state shortly after a new European Parliament has been elected. All new legislation is debated by both the *European Parliament* (made up of directly-elected MEPs voted by ordinary EU citizens) and the Council of Ministers (made up of ministers from each member state's government). Both have to agree with a piece of legislation before it can be made law. Once it has been passed, it is returned to the Commission to be put into action (normally in the form of *directives* that have to be followed). EU law takes precedence over laws decided by national governments.

Many recent reforms of the EU have aimed to give more power to the European Parliament as it is the only directly-elected institution in the EU. This is to address the argument that there is a *democratic deficit* in the EU (the idea that the EU has more power than it has democratic accountability). As well as giving the Parliament co-decision powers with the Council of Ministers, as described above (prior to the 1990s MEPs were only "consulted"), this has also given the Parliament the power to approve (or not) appointments to the Commission and the (rather dramatic) power to dismiss the entire Commission. This is sometimes called the "nuclear option" as they do not have the power to sack individual commissioners, only the institution as a whole. They have never actually used this power although they effectively did in 1999 when the Santer Commission resigned en masse in advance of the vote of censure in the Parliament. This was because of the corrupt activities of two commissioners, so many have argued that the ability to censure individual commissioners would be a sensible reform.

In or Out?

Despite these reforms, for some the EU remains an undemocratic force, for others it is essential. We may have an "in/out" referendum in the coming years (depending on the outcomes of future elections) so what are the key arguments likely to be:

The case for staying in	*The case for getting out*
Most of our trade is with the EU	Lack of democratic accountability
Many jobs are related to our EU membership (exact number is disputed)	High cost of membership
EU changes would still affect us whether we were in or not, better to be in, helping to make the rules	Impact of EU immigration on UK services and society
Many issues require international cooperation – crime, immigration, drugs, environmental issues, economic issues: all cross national borders and therefore require cooperation	Impacts freedom to trade on own terms outside EU (e.g. with the Commonwealth)
Has helped keep the peace in Europe since Second World War	Restrictions on what UK governments could choose to do (e.g. left-wing governments restricted in terms of public ownership and welfare spending; right-wing governments restricted in terms of flexible working and "cutting red tape")
We have benefited from rules on working conditions, hours, social policies, etc.	Financial cost of bailing out poorer economies in the EU, especially the failing fringes of the Eurozone

As is probably clear, not all Europhiles (those who love Europe) would use every argument on the left column and not all Eurosceptics would use every argument on the right-hand column. There are left-wing and right-wing versions of both positions. A left-wing Eurosceptic would be less concerned about immigration while a right-wing Europhile would point to the fact that the UK has been able to opt out of most of the social rules that other EU citizens have benefited from in terms of maximum working hours and minimum holidays, etc.

What do you think? Are you a Europhile or a Eurosceptic or somewhere in between? Why not organise a big debate in your school or college on the subject and consider inviting in speakers from outside to get things started. There are plenty of pro and anti EU campaigning groups out there who would be keen to engage with you.

B. Britain and other international organisations

The European Union is not the only international political organisation that the UK is a member of. Two others we will refer to briefy here (and you should investigate further) are the United Nations and NATO

Because both your exams are in the summer, you will cover lots of material relevant to the UN, NATO and political globalisation in CIST4. Be synoptic; make the links. Bring these modules together at this point.

Like the European Union, the United Nations was born out of the great political upheaval of the Second World War. A similar organisation – the League of Nations – had existed between the wars and is viewed historically as a great failure, as it was unable to prevent the activities of first Mussolini and then Hitler and, ultimately, to prevent another World War. The whole purpose of the United Nations was to prevent future war, but also to try and prevent future terrible violations of human rights within national boundaries (*see Part Two*). For the United Nations to function, all countries had to be members; all had to have voting rights in the General Assembly.

However, some members of the United Nations are more powerful than others. There are five *permanent members* of the United Nations *Security Council*. The Security Council is the essential body when it comes to issues relating to potential military activity. The United Nations *can* deploy troops in military situations as well as approve or condemn military activities by its members. These sorts of decisions are taken by the Security Council and the five permanent members are: the USA, Russia, China, France and the UK. If any one of the five permanent members of the Security Council vote against a resolution (i.e. a proposal) then they *veto* it.

Why?
Very good question. They do seem a rather odd selection of countries (at least after the first three). The reason is that, at the time of the creation of the permament members, these five

countries were the only ones to legally have nuclear weapons. The threat of nuclear war seemed so real and terrifying for much of the latter part of the 20th century that the idea of the UN approving actions against the wishes of any one of these five countries seemed unthinkable. Of course, since then India, Pakistan, Israel and (possibly) North Korea have all acquired nuclear weapons illegally and whether other countries have or are close to having developed them is a matter of some debate.

This is probably a good moment to try and explain why some countries have nuclear weapons legally and others illegally. In 1968, a UN treaty was signed: the Nuclear Non-Proliferation Treaty. This treaty committed all signatories to agree not to acquire nuclear weapons and, in exchange, the current nuclear states (i.e. the five that already had them; the five permamanet members of the security council) would agree to share nuclear technology and expertise for the development of nuclear energy and – in more recent amendments – would agree to multi-laterally scale back their own weaponry with a view to a non-nuclear future. Most agree that the treaty has been extraordinarily successful in its principal aim. In the late 60s most assumed that within a decade or so there might be 20+ nuclear states. Today there are only 5 states who are not signed up to the NPT. South Sudan is something of an anomoly (they are a very new sovereign state and one would expect them to sign in the future): the other 4 are the only "new" nuclear states: India, Pakistan, Israel and North Korea. As such, by having nuclear weapons they have not broken treaty agreements that they have themselves made, but they have gone against the clear agreement of the other 189 countries in the world. North Korea did accede to the Treaty in the 1980s but withdrew in 2003. Why have those countries flown in the face of the shared wisdom of the other 189? India and Pakistan have had their own arms race because of significant disagreements between themselves; as such each has development nuclear weapons because of their fear that the other was doing so. Israel developed nuclear weapons because of its fear of attack from some of its Arab neighbours, especially those who were themselves accused of developing weapons of mass destruction (e.g. Iraq, Iran, Syria). North Korea has a peculiar dictatorship and (along with Iraq, Iran, Libya and Syria) was named as part of an "axis of evil" by former US President George W. Bush. Other countries that have signed the Treaty have had their compliance to it questioned at times over the years (e.g. Iran). Of course, because the nuclear states have strongly defended having nuclear weapons against some popular opposition, it is hard for them to logically or morally dismantle the arguments of other nations that wish to develop them. If our Trident missiles are really what has kept the UK safe and free for decades, then why shouldn't North Korea or Iran have the same?

So Britain is a very significant member of the United Nations. The UK has used its veto in the United Nations Security Council, normally alongside the USA in preventing international condemnation of Israel's relationship with Palestine, but also, in the 1980s, in preventing condemnation of the government of Saddam Hussain in Iraq! The United Nations do develop *international law* which impacts on the government of the UK. It is international law (agreed by the UN) that says all nations should accept genuine refugees, for example, and that countries should not launch wars of aggression against other countries. United Nations agreements is one of the sources of human rights legislation adhered to in the UK. So the United Nations, which meets in New York, may seem quite a remote organisation with little impact on our lives, this is a long way from being true. The UN has been the subject of much criticism and debate, especially since the build-up to the war in Iraq in 2003. This is the subject of a later section and might be something you want to research further.

NATO stands for North Atlantic Treaty Organisation and was established to link the USA with its western-European allies in a protective alliance against Communist Russia and its allies. It was a fundamental part of the Cold War that polarised the world for much of the 20th century. Britain is a key player in NATO as one of the larger military powers in it. The USA is clearly the dominant military player, but the UK has the next most powerful military and (along with France and the US) is a nuclear power within the alliance. NATO does not impact on the day-to-day politics of the UK very much, but it is a protective treaty where, should there be a military attack on any NATO member, the UK would have a treaty obligation to take military action in its support, whatever the state of public opinion in the UK. Had Ukraine been successful in its desire to join NATO, or had Russia decided to intervene in the internal affairs of Latvia, Lithuania or Estonia in the way it did in Ukraine in 2014, the UK may well have found itself in a war it had not planned nor was in any way prepared for. In recent years, however, NATO has been a more pro-active player in international controversy, rather than reacting to attacks (NATO members have not been attacked and clearly that is an attraction to joining). NATO has instead chosen to intervene in Libya, Afghanistan and Kosovo (for example). It famously could not agree a joint position on Iraq in 2003 because France and Germany (in particular) were high profile NATO members who opposed military intervention. See Part Two for further consideration of these issues.

You might like to read up on other international bodies in which the UK plays a part, such as the Commonwealth, the IMF and the World Bank. Build a fact file and keep it with your notes.

C. Globalisation & politics

There is a section in Part Two of this book that is devoted entirely to the issue of globalisation. Please refer to that section **now** for a clear description of what is meant by globalisation and to the debates about globalisation.

In Part Two the main focus is on economic and cultural globalisation, but there is evidence of political globalisation too. Apart from anything else, it is hard to separate politics from economic, cultural and social issues. Furthermore, many political problems are international problems that require international solutions, hence of the role of bodies like the EU, the UN and NATO.

Revisit this section after you have studied globalisation in CIST4. Produce a poster, using material from CIST4 and from the rest of this BRITAIN IN THE WORLD section, considering whether there has been a significant degree of globalisation of politics since the Second World War.

Test Yourself:

1. Which UK political party was formed in 1900?
2. Which major UK political party is considered to be a "centre-right" party?
3. What is meant by the latin phrase *"primus inter pares"*?
4. What are the main roles of Parliament?
5. How many women are there in Parliament?

POLITICS, POWER AND PARTICIPATION EXAM QUESTIONS

Remember: when you think of what content to include in these essays, think about your knowledge from other modules and other subjects too. Demonstrate your ability to synthesize! Remember to make an argument. Use words and phrases like "however", "on the other hand" and "while some argue x, others suggest y" to demonstrate that you are analysing. Do not just describe.

01 Examine how MPs carry out their representative role in the House of Commons (15 marks)

02 Assess the view that there is now no real difference between the ideologies of Conservative, Labour and Liberal Democrat parties (25 marks)

OR

03 Examine the relationship between Britain and **one** key international organisation (15 marks)

04 "The British Prime Minsiter is an elected dictator" Critically evaluate this view (25 marks)

OR

05 Explain **and** comment on the role of local councillors (15 marks)

06 Assess the view that Britain should reform its electoral system and adopt a system of proportional representation for general elections (25 marks)

PART TWO: GLOBAL ISSUES AND MAKING A DIFFERENCE

HUMAN RIGHTS

The very concept of universal, inalienable human rights is far from a straightforward one. Are all humans, wherever we happen to live, imbued with the same set of rights? Or do rights come with responsibilities, as part of a "social contract" of citizenship?

The latter view was a popular and widespread one for many years, and is the definition of what we call "civil rights" but is insufficient to solve some of the great problems of the 20th century. If a government decides not to grant its people freedom but instead to intern them, transport them, kill them in huge numbers – like in Nazi Germany and other areas of Nazi-occupied Europe – the issue is surely much bigger than one of *civil rights*. If foreign nationals are attacked or tortured, do they not have some protection, despite not being citizens? The concept of human rights is a very important one then, even though it is far from an easy one.

While most agree that there should be human rights and that there are civil rights and that there will be some overlap between the two, there is a lot of disagreement.

Something like the United States' Bill of Rights is a good example of a set of Civil Rights. All citizens are entitled to an important set of rights, guaranteed in the constitution. Nobody would consider the right to bear arms a *human* right. Many argue that it shouldn't be a right at all! However, surely freedom from "cruel and unusual punishment" and the right to a fair trial should not just be considered a *civil* right but a right guaranteed to all humans regardless of citizenship?

What about democratic rights, like the right to vote? Clearly the right to vote in the elections of a specific country must be a *civil right*. We do not allow all humans, regardless of citizenship, to vote in UK elections. However, some would argue that the right to vote in general – the right to have a say in your government – should be a human right. Of course, if it is a human right, it is one that many millions of people are denied around the world.

What about social and economic rights? The right to a job? The right to shelter, clean water, food, healthcare and security? Are these human rights? If so, where there is unemployment, homelessness, hunger, poor health and insecurity (in every country in the world, to a greater or lesser extent) who is guilty of human rights abuses?

You should consider all of these questions when dealing with the issue of human rights.

You should also be aware that some people, known as cultural relativists, argue that human rights cannot be universal because you must view them in the cultural context in which you find them. Human rights as described in the European Convention on Human Rights are those that have developed in the cultural and historical context of western Europe in the 20th century, and it would be wrong to apply them in other contexts without any understanding of differences in history, values, religion and culture. Although there is undoubtedly some truth in this, others worry that it is used as an excuse for ignoring some terrible abuses and denying people in other countries the rights that we expect to enjoy ourselves. It is a difficult area.

Can you think of an example of a practice or practices that, if they were carried out on your street would be considered appalling but are considered normal and acceptable in the countries where they occur? Because they are considered normal does that mean that the apparent victims do not have the right to be protected ?

In the UK, we have the Human Rights Act (1998) that came into force in 2000. It puts into UK law the European Convention on Human Rights, to which the UK has been a signatory since 1950, when it was drafted following the Second World War. The whole point of the European Convention, and the United Nations Declaration of Human Rights (1948), is that the rights of citizens is no longer just a civil matter or a domestic matter, but is the business of the international community. The idea that all human beings have rights.

The rights established in UK law by the Human Rights Act include:

- The right to life
- The prohibition of torture and inhuman treatment
- Protection against slavery and forced labour
- The right to liberty and freedom
- The right to a fair trial and no punishment without law
- Respect for privacy and family life and the right to marry
- Freedom of thought, religion and belief
- Free speech and peaceful protest
- No discrimination
- Protection of property,
- The right to an education
- The right to free elections

What do you think? Should all human beings have all of these rights unconditionally? Remember, when you think about your answer, that all human beings includes murderers, neo-Nazis, terrorists and

Few of these rights are entirely uncontroversial. The right to life seems pretty straightforward, but there is a significant minority that would like to bring back the death sentence for the most serious crimes. There are also plenty of countries around the world which still use the death penalty, not all of whom we would think of as countries that routinely breach human rights. There are restrictions on deporting some criminals to the USA under the Human Rights Act, for example, if there is any question of those criminals facing the death penalty. Few would question the right not to be tortured – whatever crime that person might have committed – but there was a public outcry when the European Court of Human Rights concluded that Abu Qatada (a radical cleric accused of supporting Al Qaeda) could not be deported by British governments to Jordan because he had been tortured in Jordan and evidence gathered from that torture might be used in his trial. The right to marry and to family life seems quite uncontroversial, but some Christians fear that recent changes allowing gay couples to marry might lead to religious bodies being taken to human rights trials should they refuse to perform gay marriages. Also there have again been issues relating to the deportation of foreign criminals when their lawyers have shown evidence of them having established a family in the UK.

It seems that most people are happy with the concept of human rights until they apply to *some* humans in certain emotive situations.

One of the more controversial issues relating to human rights in recent years was the conclusion of the European Court of Human Rights (yet to be repeated in a British court or accepted by a British government) that the UK is breaching human rights legislation by not allowing prisoners to vote.

would that send to other countries in Europe and the world with much worse human rights records than ours?

Find some case studies of human rights abuses. For your research use the Amnesty International website and the website of the Human Rights Watch. They will give you some up-to-date case studies to consider. Do these cases mostly refer to dictatorships and countries in the developing world?

Now do some research into Guantanamo Bay. How did the USA – a modern, liberal, democratic state – justify the use of long-term imprisonment without trial and alleged torture (use of waterboarding, sleep deprivation, etc.)? Consider the same questions in relation to extraordinary rendition. *What is this?*

Also find out what happened at Abu Ghraib prison in Iraq in 2003.

Citizens use various methods to try and bring an end to human rights abuses. When it is their own rights being abused, perhaps in the UK, then the matter can be pursued through the courts, citing the Human Rights Act and the European Convention. However, when citizens wish to bring about change in relation to the human rights of others, in other parts of the world, then they do this via campaigning and through pressure groups.

From your earlier research, what campaigns are Amnesty International currently running? What methods do they use? Make links to work you did during AS Citizenship Studies relating to pressure groups

Groups also use the media to try and bring informal pressure to bear on governments that abuse human rights. Exposure of human rights abuse is a powerful weapon. When people know that rights are being abused in a country, then they can react in a variety of ways. They might be less likely to go on holiday to that country; they may boycott their exports; they might expect their own government to behave differently with that government in diplomatic situations. A television documentary about human rights abuses in Sri Lanka put pressure on several governments not to attend a Commonwealth meeting in that country, and pressure on those that did attend to raise the issue in meetings with the Sri Lankan leaders. Knowledge about apartheid in South Africa (raised through extensive campaigning) led to public boycotts of South African exports as well as government *sanctions* against the regime. Economic sanctions are imposed on certain governments by international groups, such as the United Nations, which restrict the trade that might be carried out with that country. Sometimes these are very general (such as the sanctions regime against Iraq for much of the 1990s) and other times they can be very targeted at certain individuals and goods (such as the sanctions currently – at the time of writing - being implemented against Russia in relation to the Ukraine situation).

It is argued that, if governments are aware that people are watching, they are less likely to abuse human rights. That was an essential element of the early Amnesty International campaigns whereby supporters were encouraged to write to political prisoners around the world, to show their captors that they were not forgotten and that the world was watching.

However, sometimes exposure is not enough. The world could not have been more aware of Guantanamo Bay, and President Barack Obama was brought to power on the back of a campaign that included the pledge to close the detention camp. Obama's second term is well advanced at the time of writing, and there are still detainees in Guantanamo.

TEST YOURSELF:

1. When was the Human Rights Act passed in the UK?
2. Where is the European Court of Human Rights based?
3. What is meant by cultural relativism?
4. What is extraordinary rendition?
5. Identify two recent campaigns by Amnesty International

3 CONFLICT & CONFLICT RESOLUTION

There are many conflicts around the world, some of which the UK is involved in (such as in Afghanistan) and others in which our government has no direct interest. It is the role of the global citizen to take an interest in international conflicts. War and conflicts start for a number of reasons, and often a complex mixture of reasons.

Territorial disputes are often key to conflict. The Israel-Palestine conflict is often presented as a *religious* conflict between Muslims and Jews (and clearly there is a significant religious element to the conflict) but at its heart it is a territorial conflict about the borders of Israel, the existence and viability of a Palestinian state, and the right of both nation-states to exist. Essentially, therefore, it is a *political* conflict, although religion certainly complicates things (e.g. some on the Israeli side consider the state of Israel to have been God's gift to the Jewish people and therefore do not accept any compromise regarding its borders, while some on the Palestinian side see their struggle as part of a Jihad, or Holy War, where again compromise is impossible).

The Northern Ireland troubles can also be seen in a similar context where a political dispute over territory (i.e. should Northern Ireland be Irish or British) is complicated by a religious dispute between Protestant and Catholic communities.

But there are other factors in war and conflict, beyond territory and religion. Internal conflicts or civil wars might be fought over political struggles (e.g. the wish for democracy, to remove a tyrannical regime or change a political system) as well as over ethnic or tribal disputes. Conflicts between nations can often be about the control of resources, or about broader strategic considerations (e.g. the safety of trading routes, access to sea ports, safety of key allies, etc.) There have also been conflicts in more recent times that have apparently been fought in order to protect human rights – what is described as humanitarian intervention. An often cited example of this would be UN and NATO interventions in the former Yugoslavia and also it was the justification for NATO involvement in the Libyan conflict in 2011.

It is no coincidence that many of the world's poorest regions are also war zones. Huge sums of money that might have been invested in infrastructure or spent on important resources have instead been spent on weapons of war. Essential aid and trade routes have been effectively blocked by civil war and fear of guerilla activity. Food aid has even been used as a weapon in conflicts – the Zimbabwean government was alleged to have directed food aid away from areas where people supported opposition parties, during a devastating famine.

As such, the need for conflict resolution is an overwhelming one and one that does involve all the world's citizens, not just those who are directly connected to the conflict in question.

A. Northern Ireland

The roots of the Northern Irish conflict are centuries old. Those citizenship students who have also studied A Level History might well have done some Irish history. For the rest of you, only a fairly brief overview of the background to the conflict is necessary, but you might wish to research it further.

The whole of the island of Ireland was, for many years, part of the United Kingdom. There was a long history of Irish Nationalism – a political movement that wanted to establish Ireland as a separate nation. Although at various times in history there were both Roman Catholic and Protestant Irish nationalists, the nationalist cause was certainly stronger among the Catholic majority. When Irish nationalism became increasingly popular in the twentieth century, the strongest opposition to it was among the Protestant population in Ulster (the northern province of Ireland) who feared being a religious minority in an independent, Catholic Ireland.

Politicians in Britain were divided between unionists (most notably in the Conservative Party) and those who supported Home Rule for Ireland (including many in the Liberal and Labour parties). In Easter 1916 there was an uprising in Dublin. A small number of committed, armed Republicans attempted a revolution. It was put down speedily and bloodily. It had not been popular even in nationalist areas of Ireland, as it was at the height of the First World War when many Irishmen were fighting for the Allies in France and elsewhere. But the treatment of the leaders of the uprising (several were summarily shot) caused a sea change in public opinion. Within a few years Irish nationalism was a popular cause and the IRA a fast-growing, effective and deadly guerilla organisation. In 1922 the British government finally decided to seek a compromise and proposed a Treaty that would grant Home Rule to *most* of Ireland, leaving a province in the north (*most* of Ulster) under British jurisdiction.

A civil war ensued in Ireland between those who supported the Treaty and those who wanted to hold out and fight for a united Ireland. It ended with the assassination of the pro-Treaty, IRA leader Michael Collins. When Ireland became a Republic in the 1960s, it enshrined its claim to the north in its constitution. In Northern Ireland, the devolved government in Belfast had an inbuilt Protestant majority and for many years the rights of Catholics in the province were severely curtailed. As such, while politics in the Republic of Ireland slowly "normalized", politics in the North remained deeply sectarian, the IRA remained an active force in the Catholic community, as did "loyalist" paramilitary groups that had developed in the Protestant community.

The British troops were originally sent into Northern Ireland to protect the Catholic minority, but – especially after Bloody Sunday (*read up about these events*) – found themselves the targets of attacks from the new Provisional IRA. This organisation also attacked targets in mainland Britain, with assassinations and bombings. Meanwhile, loyalist paramilitaries were themselves engaging in ever more sectarian killings and attacks on Catholic communities.

Paramilitary prisoners considered themselves to be political prisoners, or prisoners of war, and therefore protested against being treated as normal criminals. IRA Hunger Strikes led to international outrage, especially when Bobby Sands – a Sinn Fein MP and IRA activist – starved to death.

It became increasingly clear to governments that there was no military solution to the Northern Ireland troubles. Successive governments sought to find a negotiated settlement. At the same time, the political wing of the Republican movement also saw that a military solution was not possible. They could not bomb their way to a united Ireland any more than the British government could shoot, incarcerate and legislate their way to an end to IRA violence.

Ultimately it was moderate nationalist leader John Hume, together with the Sinn Fein leader Gerry Adams, who came forward with a peace proposal. Together with Ulster Unionist leader David Trimble, the government of the Republic of Ireland and first John Major and later (and more successfully) Tony Blair, they put together a peace plan that ultimately brought the Troubles to an end. There are still problems in Northern Ireland and sectarian violence remains, but the change since the 1970s and 1980s is astonishing.

So what did they do?

It certainly was not an easy process. All parties had to make compromises and the communities or constituencies for each party had to see that everybody else was compromising as much as they were. This proved very difficult indeed.

All parties had to sign up to a general agreement. This was called the Good Friday Agreement, of 1998. Initially, one of the Unionist parties (the DUP, now the biggest party in Northern Ireland) did not sign up. The population of Northern Ireland also voted on the agreement in a referendum and both communities gave their consent (although there were significant minorities on both sides that did not support the peace process). The people of the Republic of Ireland also had a referendum, to give up their historic constitutional claim on Northern Ireland – they did vote to give this up.

Major difficulties included the decommissioning of weapons. All paramilitary groups who had signed up to the process were expected to put their weapons beyond use. There were symbolic issues relating to this (e.g. the IRA handing their weapons over to a UK government body would be a symbolic "surrender"). Furthermore while the UK government saw the decommissioning of IRA and loyalist weapons as "equivalent", the IRA saw the withdrawal of British troops as the "equivalent" to them disarming. This led to a major stumbling block.

Other problems related to the future of policing in the province. The nationalist community had seen the old police force (the RUC) as very much a sectarian, Protestant force. Sinn Fein in particular was very concerned that the new Northern Ireland police force should be seen to have been radically reformed.

Perhaps the most difficult parts of the conflict resolution process related to the release of prisoners and the "truth and reconciliation" commission. This latter approach was borrowed from South Africa where, following the end of apartheid, public apologies, explanations and displays of anger and remorse were seen as an important part of the national healing process. In Northern Ireland this presented itself in the form of terrorists meeting with the families of victims and trying to explain their actions, while the families of victims told of their pain and loss. In some cases it included revealing the location of the bodies of some of the "disappeared".

The early release of prisoners was, of course, particularly painful for victims and victims' families.

So, the Northern Ireland Peace Process involved:

- A peace plan
- The intervention of international peace envoys (including heads of state like US President Bill Clinton)
- Bringing the public along with the process (through referendums)
- A political process – a big part of the peace process was devolution to a Northern Ireland Assembly and cross-community power-sharing executive
- Decommissioning of weapons and demilitarization
- Truth and reconciliation
- An attempt to include all interested parties in talks and solutions.

The Northern Ireland peace process is an example of conflict resolution being *successful*.

B. Iraq

The origins of the Iraq War and the reasons for it are a matter of some debate. Whether there will one day be consensus among historians as to exactly what caused the war, nobody can say, but for now we need to consider the facts as we currently know them and a variety of theories regarding the motives of various players.

Iraq was led by a ruthless and internationally unpopular dictatorship, headed by Saddam Hussain. Saddam was a long-serving president and had been an unlikely ally of Western powers during the long and bloody Iran-Iraq War in the 1980s, when western countries had backed the more secular Iraq against the Islamist Iran.

It was widely known that both sides in the Iran-Iraq War developed – and used – chemical weapons and Iraq was also known to be developing biological weapons. The technology for producing these weapons was purchased all around the world, including from the UK and US governments as well as the Soviet Union. Towards the end of the Iran-Iraq War, Iraq used chemical weapons against its own people at Halabja, an act that was widely condemned.

But it was Iraq's invasion of small but wealthy neighbour Kuwait that turned it into a "rogue" or "pariah" state. Whatever Saddam's reason for invading Kuwait (to secure oil prices or to establish more sea ports) it enraged Kuwait's ally, the USA – led by George Bush Senior.

This led to the First Gulf War, in which Saddam's forces were quickly and ignominiously defeated. The ceasefire that ended that war put a number of restrictions on the Iraqi government. These included "no fly zones" in the North and South of the country (policed by NATO aircraft) and a very strict *sanctions* regime. This presented itself in terms of very strict restrictions on imports and exports in Iraq, especially relating to any items that might be used in the manufacture of weapons. But the other big demand on Iraq, in order to secure the ceasefire, was that it should disarm itself of Weapons of Mass Destruction (WMD). United Nations weapons inspectors came to the country and oversaw the destruction of large quantities of chemical and biological weapons and the technology to make them.

Iraqi officials did not make this easy! They were regularly accused of hiding things from the inspectors. In 1998, the UN weapons inspectors were withdrawn from Iraq to allow a widespread bombing campaign by NATO aircraft. The targets that were bombed were mostly suspected weapons sites that UN inspectors had been prevented from visiting. The Iraqi government argued that some UN inspectors had been spies, finding targets for NATO attacks, thus making it much harder to agree the return of inspectors. They did not return until 2002.

What happened between 1998 and 2002?

The answer is that not an awful lot happened in Iraq, other than regular NATO bombing in the no-fly zones. The significant events elsewhere were that George W. Bush came to power in the US (with a number of his father's old colleagues by his side). There was certainly some sense of "unfinished business" in relation to Iraq. And on September 11th 2001, there was the attack on the Twin Towers.

The attack on the Twin Towers had nothing to do with Iraq. Al Qaeda's leadership was based in Afghanistan and the attackers themselves were mostly from Saudi Arabia. Nevertheless, even before the start of the Afghan war, some were talking about an attack on Iraq.

Quite how Iraq became the subject of so much international attention in 2002/3 is unclear. UK Prime Minister, Tony Blair, said that his big fear was the idea of terrorists, like those involved in the September 11th attacks, somehow getting hold of chemical, biological or even nuclear weapons. The way that could theoretically happen was if a "rogue" state, like Iraq or North Korea, developed them and chose to sell them on. George W. Bush went further, identifying an "axis of Evil" in the world, including Afghanistan (under the Taliban), Iraq (under Saddam), Iran, Libya and North Korea.

US security officers did claim some loose connection between Al Qaeda and the Iraqi government although this was never substantiated and seemed unlikely to many, as Iraq was seen as a secular and un-Islamic regime by the fundamentalists in Al Qaeda.

According to Tony Blair, an increasingly worrying amount of intelligence came across his desk in relation to Iraq's secret hoard of chemical and biological weapons. US and UK intelligence officers also became aware of an apparent attempt by Iraq to get hold of nuclear materials.

The difficulty here is that, after the Iraq War in 2003, no weapons of mass destruction were ever found and it became increasingly evident that the weapons that had existed had either been destroyed when they were meant to be, after the Gulf War, or – in some cases – had simply deteriorated and become non-lethal due to poor quality or poor storage. The apparent evidence of developing new weapons seems to have been entirely illusory.

Now it's time for a "who do you believe?" moment. The various explanations for this run like this:

- Western governments, especially the US and UK governments, had decided they were going to go to war with Iraq and therefore "sexed up" intelligence to ensure that the war would get the necessary public support
- For whatever reason (perhaps political pressure) intelligence officers presented poor, unsubstantiated or potentially entirely made-up evidence as being compelling and worrying
- There was an overwhelming consensus among all foreign security services that Iraq had weapons of mass destruction so they just assumed it was true, despite the lack of evidence
- Iraqi dissidents and exiles were so keen to remove the awful Saddam regime that they invented intelligence and fed it to security officials who took them at their word

- The Iraqi regime, sensing the game was up and that they would lose the war, quickly destroyed all their weapons in an attempt to score a public relations victory in the aftermath of the war
- The Iraqi regime thought that weapons of mass destruction would deter an attack from the West and therefore encouraged the West to believe there were hidden weapons and therefore they posed a greater threat than they really did.

Which of these explanations seems most convincing? They are not mutually exclusive, of course. Some Iraqi dissidents have openly admitted to having misled Western security officials in order to encourage regime change. However, intelligence should be subject to a great number of checks and balances before it is used to justify military action, so it would appear that people (whether it be security officials or politicians) were very happy to receive such information and were not so concerned whether or not it was true!

The other controversy surrounding the Iraq War was the extent to which plans were in place for what might happen after the initial conflict. Rather like the first Gulf War, the initial phase of fighting was over quickly. The difference this time was that the regime fell. The immediate aftermath was a great power vacuum in the country and a lack of security and law and order. There followed a large spate of looting and general criminality. However, within a short time other problems emerged. Guerilla groups fought the US and UK soldiers. Some of these were groups still loyal to the old regime, but there were new people too, including Al Qaeda supporters. Also some of Saddam's opponents also fought against the Western troops (including supporters of the radical Shia cleric, Al Sadr, the so-called Mehdi Army). What is more, these groups started fighting each other and sectarian divisions that had clearly existed under Saddam, erupted into acts of terrorism between Sunni and Shia.

Suddenly troops who had entered Iraq as part of an occupying force, gaining swift victory over a weak regime, were in a wholly different kind of conflict, acting as both peacekeepers in a civil conflict and – from the perspective of some Iraqis – an unwanted invading force.

C. Afghanistan

Afghanistan has been one of the most war-torn countries in the history of the world, and it is no coincidence that it is also one of the poorest countries on the planet. Afghanistan's strategic location on the mountains, between the Indian subcontinent and Europe, has led to it being regularly occupied. In 2001, Afghanistan was led by the Taliban. This was a group of ultra-conservative Islamists who had gained the upper hand against some of the other Mujahadeen fighters who had successfully removed the Soviet Union from the country.

Among the fighters who had removed the Soviets were foreign, Arab fighters. Foremost among them was Osama Bin Laden who, once victory over the Soviet Union was secured, turned his attention to his former allies, the USA. Their crime, from Bin Laden's perspective, was the presence of their troops in holy land in Saudi Arabia. The role of Afghanistan in this was simply a base. Afghanistan fitted the description of a "failed state" and provided a location for training camps. Al Qaeda simply means "the base".

The Taliban had powerful opponents who wished above all to remove them from power – known as the Northern League – and therefore were keen to also have powerful allies. Al Qaeda was a well-funded and highly skilled ally for the Taliban.

Life in Afghanistan under Taliban rule was miserable, especially for women who were forbidden from working or studying and had to completely cover themselves behind burkas in public. Under Soviet occupation and Soviet-backed secular governments, women had risen to significant levels in public life and many highly-qualified and experienced women had to completely change their lives when the Taliban took over. Many other aspects of life were strictly controlled, including music and entertainment.

The Taliban's religious zeal also led to them destroying ancient monuments in the country that were associated with other religions, including great statues of Buddha.

The reason for the NATO attack on Afghanistan was not to liberate women, however, it was a direct response to the September 11th attacks on the Twin Towers in New York in 2001. These attacks were swiftly identified as having been carried out by Al Qaeda. This group, and most notably its leader Osama Bin Laden, was in Afghanistan.

The Taliban were given an ultimatum: to hand over Bin Laden or face attack. Whether the Taliban were ever in a position to hand over Bin Laden is unclear – although the Taliban were the leaders of the nation, Al Qaeda was much more wealthy and powerful. In any event, Bin Laden was not handed over and the war on Afghanistan began.

Initially, the western allies gave their support to the Northern League, clearing the way for them with bombing raids. The capital Kabul fell relatively quickly, but Taliban resistance has remained ever since. At the time of writing, the Afghan War has been continuing for nearly thirteen years, longer than the First and Second World Wars combined. As in Iraq, the role of international troops has changed to one of peace-keeping and training. The mission for UK troops continues to be extremely dangerous with regular British casualties.

Increasingly politicians have talked about the need to open up negotiation with the Taliban, something that would have been considered out of the question ten years ago.

D. Syria

This conflict is very much still on-going at the time of writing.

It began, like the Libya conflict before it, as part of the *Arab Spring*.

The Arab Spring was a name given to a series of uprisings in the Arab world, starting in the spring of 2011. The initial successes of uprisings in Tunisia and Egypt led to a great deal of optimism. However, in places like Bahrain (for example), the regimes were able to maintain their rigid command (with assistance from Saudi Arabia) and in Libya and Syria, uprisings quickly transformed into Civil War.

In Libya, the international community chose to intervene. UK Prime Minister, David Cameron, and then French President Nicolas Sarkozy both made strong statements and committed themselves to military intervention. NATO backed the Libyan rebel fighters, carrying out airstrikes to help them to eventual victory against the Gadaffi regime. Even with this mighty support from the air (and some quiet support on the ground) the civil war raged on for many months.

The argument given for military intervention, as opposed to a diplomatic approach was to prevent a humanitarian catastrophe: a feared assault by the regime on the Libyan city of Benghazi, which was the stronghold of the opposition.

The Syrian uprising was met with a brutal response from the the Assad regime. Like in Libya it quite quickly developed from uprising to civil war. But unlike in Libya there was no military response from the international community, even after some high profile atrocities, and the fighting escalated beyond anything seen in Libya. Instead, the response from the international community was a diplomatic one. Unfortunately, it was not faster in bringing things to a conclusion than the military approach in Libya had been.

In 2013 the US and its allies came close to intervening militarily after evidence emerged of the use of chemical weapons during the conflict. Had it not been for the experience of the Iraq War it is very likely that military intervention would have occurred. However, in the UK, the Labour Party voted against military intervention in Syria and, together with government rebels, defeated David Cameron in Parliament. Perhaps surprisingly, the USA also decided against intervention once it was clear that they would not have the support of the UK. The conflict is still ongoing at the time of writing.

E. Ukraine

Finally, this is a conflict that is absolutely current as I write. However, it appears to be a potentially very useful one for a study of certain methods of conflict resolution and also of the weakness of some international bodies to deal with some issues.

The United Nations has been unable to reach a united view on Ukraine, for example, because Russia is a permanent member of the Security Council and wields a veto.

NATO and the European Union have taken clearer positions on the conflict, condemning Russia and, in the case of the EU, imposing sanctions. Even here there is some inconsistency because different countries have different relationships with Russia, particularly economic relationships. One thing that nobody appears to be contemplating in this situation is military intervention: Russia, of course, really does have weapons of mass destruction…

Build a fact file on Ukraine. Find out about the Euromaidan protests in 2013, the coup d'etat of 2014 and the developments in Crimea and East Ukraine. Make sure you read about the Russian version of events too. Consider which side of the argument you find most convincing. Keep up to date with changes as they occur.

War Crimes Tribunals and Trials:
At the end of the Iraq War, Saddam Hussain was put on trial in Iraq, found guilty and hanged. (His hanging was filmed on a mobile phone and "went viral" on the internet). At the end of the Libyan conflict, Gadaffi was found, dragged through a street and killed. However, sometimes leaders and those accused of war criminals are tried in international courts. Examples include trials in the International Criminal Court (ICC) of those accused of war crimes in the former Yugoslavia. Why not find out all you can about the trials of Radovan Karadžić and Slobodan Milošević.. What do these stories tells us about the success or otherwise of these sorts of tribunals?

Test Yourself:

1. What year was the Good Friday Agreement signed in Northern Ireland?
2. Why did NATO bomb Afghanistan in 2001?
3. Who was Slobodan Milošević?
4. Why do some people think Crimea is rightly part of Russia?
5. What is meant by *economic sanctions?*

THE ENVIRONMENT

One of the most significant issues relating to global citizenship in recent years has been the issue of global warming. Climate change has become the enironmental issue of greatest global concern in recent times (though it is far from being the only international environmental issue) and it is also a matter of some controversy.

Global environmental issues include:

- Deforestation (what's this?)
- Desertification
- Pollution (many different kinds)
- Destruction of habitats
- Flooding
- Climate change
- Issues relating to animals and animal rights

Which do you think are the most significant environmental issues facing the world today?
Justify your decision
What is currently being done to deal with this? Is it working? What else could be done?
Write your findings up as a short project and keep in your notes.

Environmental politics are often described as *green*. There are different "shades of green" to describe different approaches.

Light green is the term given to an environmental politics that is quite moderate and proposes realistic changes in government policy alongside minor lifestyle changes as the solution to environmental problems. Light green thinking would recommend supporting recycling, cycling, energy-saving lightbulbs, etc.

Dark green thinking, on the other hand, is much more radical – even extreme. At the darkest end of dark green thinking, there is a view that economic growth and development needs to be reversed. Cars should perhaps be banned; people should have complete lifestyle changes. Their solutions are ecocentric rather than anthrocentric: i.e. saving the planet for the sake of the planet, not for the sake of the people (whom they are likely to think are doomed anyway!) This approach might include some of the more radical animal rights activists. Sometimes people use the term environmentalism (light green) and ecologism (dark green) to differentiate between these views.

There is also *bright green* thinking which, like dark green thinking, considers light green solutions to be inadequate, but is much more optimistic than the dark green view. People sometimes use the term "lite green" in a pejorative sense to criticise those that use environmentalism purely as a marketing strategy without any genuine commitment to environmental protection.

Try and find a copy of the film "An Inconvenient Truth" by former US Vice President Al Gore (it is available online). It gives a compelling "Bright Green" argument about man-made climate change and solutions to it. However, there are lots of critical essays online about the film. Read some of these too in order to understand the controversy.

TRADE & GLOBALISATION

Globalisation is the idea that the world is getting smaller. Not physically, of course, but economically, socially, culturally and politically. Increasingly we live in "one world", a "global village" where what happens in other countries has profound effects on our lives. In many ways, that is what this whole module is about. We need concern ourselves with "global citizenship" because we can no longer only concern ourselves with all things British. The globalisation idea rests on significant and fundamental changes in the world in the last fifty years or so. We can communicate with people on the other side of the planet, instantly; we can travel anywhere; we can do business with (nearly) anybody, anywhere. Various global issues affect us all: environmental matters, the economy, immigration, the drugs trade, terrorism, etc. and therefore where solutions are needed, they must also be *international* or involve widespread agreement between countries. There would be little point one country having a strong set of policies against pollution if all their neighbours polluted as much as ever.

There are a variety of responses to the idea of globalisation. First of all there are…

Globalists. Globalists believe in globalisation. They can be divided into *hyper-globalists* and *pessimistic globalists*. Hyper-globalists believe that globalisation is happening and that this is overwhelmingly a good and positive thing. They believe that global trade is a modernising influence everywhere, and that we are all more knowledgeable, tolerant and understanding of the world around us as a result of our shrinking planet.

Pessimistic globalists believe that globalisation is happening but think that it is overwhelmingly negative and damaging. They see cultural globalisation as *westernization* or cultural imperialism. They see global trade as entirely favouring the rich – particularly in the wealthy nations - while importing poverty and oppression to the rest of the world. They would point to people in the developing world being paid next to nothing in appalling conditions in order to produce cheap and convenient consumer goods for the West.

Then there are…

Traditionalists. These people (often coming from a Marxist perspective, not entirely dissimilar to pessimistic globalists) do not think that globalisation is really happening. They do not feel that anything particularly new or significant is occurring, it is just part of the world capitalist system that has existed for hundreds of years, as described in the writings of Karl Marx!

Finally, there are *transformationalists* who believe that globalisation is happening, but that it is not inevitable. They argue that nation states can decide which parts of globalisation they like and stop and reverse those parts that they consider damaging or against their interests.

The two that it's most worth being aware of for the purposes of your Citizenship A Level are the two types of globalists, although you should also be aware that globalisation is "just a theory".

So, there are a variety of *types* of globalisation:

Political globalisation. International organisations are increasingly important, politically. Some decisions have to be taken above national level, so we have organisations like the United Nations and also the European Union. See the above section on "Britain and the World" for further details.

Cultural globalisation. This is the idea that we increasingly experience and consume *global culture* rather than, say, British culture or Egyptian culture. For some this is all about Westernization and homogenization, whereas others say that there is an increasingly pluralistic culture everywhere, and we in the west can experience "World culture" just as much as the rest of the world gets to hear western pop music and watch the Simpsons...

Economic globalisation. This is the most relevant to this module. This is the idea that we are increasingly becoming one world economy; a global capitalist system where the economic policies of individual governments have little impact.

There are two key theories about global development that are relevant here: *Modernisation Theory* and *Dependency Theory*.

Modernisation Theory is an essentially *conservative* theory, developed from policy advisors in the USA who were concerned about the appeal of communism to the poorest people in the world. A key figure was **Walt Rostow**. Rostow wrote "The Stages of Economic Growth: A Non-Communist Manifesto" in 1960 that set out **five stages** that all countries can develop through in order to become developed.

1. **Traditional Society** Largely agricultural societies, with high levels of *subsistance*, with traditional belief systems, and old-fashioned "collective" values
2. **Preparing for Take-Off** Farmers start making profits and investing them in new science, etc. (For the UK this was thanks to natural resources, etc. but for modern developing societies this might require aid and investment from developed countries)
3. **Take off** Industrialisation

4. **Drive to maturity** Modernisation, technology, etc.
5. **The age of mass consumption** Development of a modern developed society like the USA or the UK in the mid 20th century

Rostow argued that, providing countries follow the right policies (and embrace Western capitalism) they can all become developed. There are a number of key criticisms. One is that, if all countries developed in the way the UK developed, the impact on the environment would be catastrophic! Imagine all those factories, cars, quarries and mines, etc.

A bigger criticism came from the Marxist left-wing, particularly via Andre Gunter Frank and his *Dependency Theory*. Frank believed that, far from the west trying to help the developing world through aid and investment, in fact rich countries had *deliberately* kept poor countries poor so that they could get rich.

Frank argued that the missing ingredients in Rostow's five stages of economic growth were slavery and empire. The rich countries got rich thanks to taking over large parts of the world and exploiting their people and resources, as well as kidnapping people and getting them to work for them for no money. This is how the rich in the countries that are now developed got the capital they needed to invest in their burgeoning industries. But this is not just a history lesson: Frank argued that those colonial relationships were maintained, even after most of the colonies had achieved independence, through global capitalism. He even argued that international aid was part of this process: the poorer countries could be controlled by making access to aid conditional on certain political and economic reforms.

Many globalists would say that both Rostow and Frank are outdated in their theories and would argue that today there is a great deal of *interdependence* and interconnectedness between all the countries in the world.

Some acronyms that are used to describe levels of development in the world today are:
MEDC – Most economically developed countries
LEDCs – Less economically developed countries
LLEDCs – Least economically developed countries
FCCs – Former communist countries
NICs – Newly-industrialised countries.
Feminists also talk about the Fourth World (women) and the Fifth World (women in LLEDCs). For the most part these acronyms are preferable to outdated terms like First World, Second World and Third World.

Test yourself:

1. What is deforestation?
2. What is the link between carbon emissions and climate change?
3. Name a significant modernisation theorist
4. Name a significant dependency theorist
5. What does LEDC stand for?

GLOBAL ISSUES EXAM QUESTIONS

01 Explain **and** comment on the use of sanctions as a method of resolving international conflicts (15 marks)

02 "Globalisation has been overwhelmingly positive for the world." Critically evaluate this view (25 marks)

OR

03 Examine the effectiveness of citizens' campaigns to bring about change in relation to human rights (15 marks)

04 Critically assess the work of citizens or groups in dealing with **one** key environmental issue (25 marks)

OR

05 Examine the role of **one** international body in preventing and resolving conflict (15 marks)

06 Assess the view that human rights abuse is largely a developing world problem (25 marks)

ACTIVE CITIZENSHIP: "HOW TO" GUIDE

The one part of A2 Citizenship that can really play very little part in a textbook is the second half of the second module. This "active citizenship" element is very different from the one in AS, but the topic is not determined until the year is well underway. Pre-release material is available to colleges and schools, and a topic is chosen from a choice of two.

While it is hard to predict what the topic might be, it will relate to a campaigning organisation of some sort. Previous topics have included the Stop the War Coalition, the Co-operative Bank, Transition Towns, the campaign for votes at 16, the UK Youth Parliament, the Citizens Advice Bureau, the National Citizens Service and the Occupy movement.

The purpose of this section is not to try and second-guess what topics might come up, but to consider the sorts of questions that might arise and how to prepare for them.

So, whatever the organisation or group you are studying, consider:

- What do they stand for?
- When did they start? Why? Was there a specific reason? Was there a specific "founder"?
- Do they have members? A leader?
- Do they have internal democracy? (i.e. do members vote for leaders, policies, etc)
- How well funded are they? Where do they get any money from?
- What sort of people support them? Do they appeal to a particular section of society? Is their cause of particular interest to a certain section of society?
- What campaigns have they been involved with?
- What methods did they use in these campaigns?
- How are they presented in the media?
- Do they make good use of the media?
- Are there any slogans or advertising straplines associated with the movement/group/organization?
- Were you aware of the group before studying them for this module?
- What about your friends? How successfully have they raised awareness about their cause?
- How effective have they been at meeting their aims?

Okay, another important thing to consider is *synthesis*. It is very likely that the group that you have been given is one that campaigns on issues of great relevance to one or more areas you have studied during your Citizenship course.

- Identify those areas of potential synthesis
- Revise that area again, making the links to the group
- How does this group's activities relate to your own active citizenship? Have you been involved in the group? Would you consider it? (Do you support their cause?) Have you done anything similar? If so, what? If not, why?

Ultimately, if you answer all these questions in the form of a project on the group in question, you will have all the ingredients for writing two excellent essays on the subject in the exam. Make sure you have some facts to hand (e.g. when they were formed, or where they carried out one of their famous campaigns) but particularly be ready to make an argument. Were they effective? Might there have been better ways to achieve the same ends? Is there any particular controversy or debate surrounding the group in question? If so, it is quite likely that this might form an important part of one of the questions.

TIP:
Look at past papers and see the sorts of questions that have been asked as 15 and 25 mark questions in the past. Consider how the same question might be applied to the group you have been asked to research and plan an answer.

GLOSSARY

Act
Once a piece of legislation (a new law) has been approved by both houses of Parliament and has been signed by the monarch (royal assent) it ceases to be a *bill* and becomes an *Act of Parliament*, on "the statute book": law.

Additional Member System
This is a voting system used in the devolved assemblies in Scotland and Wales. This voting system combines *"first past the post"* and a proportional representation system (*party list*).

Alternative Vote
Alternative vote is another voting system, that was proposed as an alternative to *first past the post* for UK general elections. The proposal was defeated in a *referendum* in 2011.

Bill
Until a piece of legislation (a new law) is passed by Parliament and becomes an *Act*, it is called a *Bill*.

Chivalry Thesis
This is a theory that attempts to explain why statistics suggest women commit fewer crimes than men. It suggests that (predominantly) male law enforcement officers may choose not to prosecute women offenders out of a sense of gentlemanliness!

Conservatism
This is an ideology (or group ideologies) associated with the Conservative Party in the UK. Literally it simply refers to a perspective that wishes to preserve things as they are or to change things slowly (as opposed to radicalism that wants rapid change). However, it has evolved over time and now there are a range of conservative ideas, e.g. traditional conservatism, one nation conservatism, new right conservatism, etc.

Copenhagen Treaty
The Copenhagen Treaty was an international treaty in 2009, resulting in the Copenhagen Accord that, committing countries to legally-binding targets on carbon emissions (following on from the earlier *Kyoto Treaty*). This was under UN auspices but some felt it ended up weak because of reluctance from countries like China to sign up to challenging, legally-binding targets.

Corporate Crime
This refers to crimes that are committed by companies/organisation. This might include fraud, insider trading, negligence, pollution, etc. Some oft-cited examples were not actually illegal in

the time and place where they happened, though they would have been illegal in the company's home country.

Crown Court
Criminal cases that are considered too serious to be entirely prosecuted in a magistrates' court (known as indictable offences rather than summary offences) are tried at the Crown Court in front of judge and jury.

Crown Prosecution Service
The CPS works with the police to ensure that there is sufficient evidence to bring a charge against a suspected criminal. The CPS needs to consider whether a charge would be in the public interest and whether any court case was likely to result in a successful prosecution.

Cultural Relativism
Cultural relativism is the idea that practices and ideas around the world exist in their particular social context and no particular culture or society is superior to another. It is, in that sense, the opposite of *universalism*, in that cultural relativists would argue that western values cannot be directly applied to other cultures. It presents a challenge to the concept of universal human rights.

Democracy
Literally means government by the people. Practically, it tends to refer to governments that involve free and fair elections for significant parts of the legislature and executive.

Direct Democracy
Direct democracy refers to people making political decisions *themselves* rather than *indirectly* via representatives. This would normally be through the use of a *referendum* although in smaller-scale situations could be through public meetings, etc.

Dark Green
Environmental ideas can be described in terms of *shades of green* with moderate environmentalism being *light green* and more radical ecologism being *dark green*. This is quite a radical approach to environmentalism that is ecocentric rather than anthropocentric (meaning it puts the needs of the environment ahead of the needs of humans). They often argue for veganism, alternative lifestyles and radical actions like banning cars.

Durkheim (Emile)
Emile Durkheim was a famous sociologist, often seen as the founding father of *functionalism*. He argued that crime was *functional* (i.e. was socially useful) and normal (i.e. you would expect to see some in all societies).

ECHR
The European Convention on Human Rights was established by the Council of Europe, written in 1950 and formalised in 1953. The Council of Europe is *not* related to the European Union and involves many more countries. Both the Council and the Convention were established following the Second World War in order to try and prevent something like the holocaust from happening again.

Ecologism
A name sometimes given to the *dark green* ideology; this approach distances itself from other political perspectives that are all focused on economic growth (suffering from "growthmania") rather than putting the needs of the planet first.

Environmentalism
Environmentalism is a general "catch-all" term for green politics, but is often associated with the more moderate "light green" side of the green movement.

Envoy
An envoy is somebody who works on behalf of others, normally as a *diplomat*.

EU
The European Union is a *supranational* organisation with a number of institutions (such as the European Parliament, European Commission, Council of Ministers, European Court of Justice)

First Past the Post
This is the voting system used in general elections in the UK and many other elections around the world. It is also known as *simple plurality* and works on the basis that the candidate who gets the most votes wins, regardless of what proportion of votes that they receive (i.e. they do not need to have a majority).

Genocide
Is the mass killing of all or part of a particular ethnic, racial, religious or national group. The term is sometimes misused to mean all mass killings, but the concept of genocide does specifically refer to something that is *not* indiscriminate. The classic example would be Hitler's "final solution" against the Jews.

Guantanamo Bay
Guantanamo Bay is an area on the island of Cuba (but not part of the *Republic of Cuba*) – it is run by the US government. In this area there is a US military prison camp called Camp Delta (previously Camp X-Ray).

Human Rights Act
This piece of legislation, passed in 1998 and enacted from 2000, incorporated the *European Convention on Human Rights* into UK law.

Indirect Democracy
Indirect democracy is the same as *representative democracy* and is based on the idea that it is impractical for everybody to make all decisions directly; instead they elect representatives to make those decisions for them (e.g. people in the UK vote for MPs to make decisions in the House of Commons).

Industrialisation
The development of industry; the growth of factories, etc. as opposed to agricultural economic activity. Associated with the industrial revolution in the UK and many western societies, but also with development and "modernisation" in LEDCs.

Kyoto Treaty
The Kyoto Treaty or Protocol was an international treaty signed by nearly 200 countries, under the auspices of the United Nations, in 1997 and came into force in 2005. It committed the signatories to challenging targets for reducing their emissions of greenhouse gases. Famously the United States did not ratify the Treaty after being an initial signatory, and developing countries (including some of the biggest polluters such as China) did not have binding targets. This has undermined the authority of the Treaty.

Liberalism
Liberalism is an ideology based on *rights* and *freedom*. The key principal of liberalism was described by John Stuart Mill as being that everybody has the right to do whatever they like so long as it does not infringe somebody else's freedom. There are different types of liberalism as some have focused entirely on freedom from the state (or government) and argue for minimal or limited government, whereas others see a role for government in empowering people to exercise their freedom.

Light green
Light green refers to a moderate environmentalism, where changes can be made by reasonably simple government legislation and minor lifestyle changes (e.g. improved public transport and recycling facilities and using energy-saving lightbulbs). Critics suggest that its proposed solutions are insufficient and does little more than pay lip service to the environment. (The term "lite green" is used for when environmentalism is just used as a marketing strategy).

Magistrates Court
A magistrates court is a local court chaired by lay magistrates rather than a judge. All criminal cases begin in a magistrates court for the first hearing.

Mandate

A politician has a mandate – i.e. legitimate authority – if they have been properly elected. Alternatively, a referendum might lend politicians a mandate to make a particular decision. In a democracy it is important to be able to show that the people have consented to give government authority. Therefore if a government does something that was not in their manifesto (and therefore nobody voted for it) people might question their mandate. Similarly minority governments or referendums passed on very low turnouts can be said to lack a mandate.

Marginalisation Theory

This is a feminist theory (actually a Marxist-Feminist theory) that seeks to explain the position of women in the developing world. Marginalisation theorists suggest that European empires imposed *patriarchy* onto the developing world. As a result women because increasingly marginalised, acquiring a domestic and subservient role as was the norm in Europe at the time but had not necessarily been the norm in developing countries. (This western patriarchy sometimes worked together with patriarchal cultural norms in the developing countries themselves).

Marxism

Marxism is a term used to describe the socialist/communist ideas of the hugely influential German thinker, Karl Marx. His theory was based on his analysis of capitalist society and the existence of a class struggle within society. He argued that the working-class majority had to defeat the ruling-class minority in order to establish a better (socialist) society.

Proportional Representation

Proportional representation is a term used to describe any of a range of voting systems that seek to ensure that the proportion of votes received by parties is broadly reflected in the number of seats that those parties gain in the parliament or other representative body.

NATO

North Atlantic Treaty Organisation. This was set up after the Second World War as part of the Cold War. Western Europe and the USA worked together as NATO while the Eastern Bloc communist countries formed the Warsaw Pact. Since the end of the Cold War, NATO has tried to establish a new role playing an active part in conflicts such as intervention in former Yugoslavia, Afghanistan and Libya. NATO famously could not reach agreement over Iraq (France and Germany are NATO members who were strongly opposed to military intervention in Iraq).

Neo-conservatism

Neo-conservatism is a term used to refer to modern conservative politics. It often refers to foreign policy (such as that of US President George W. Bush) but can also refer to a modern version of conservative social policies (e.g. traditional family values, strong on law and order, tough on immigration, etc.)

Neo-liberalism

Neo-liberalism refers to today's version of classical liberalism, focusing on the importance of free markets. It combines with neo-conservatism to produce the politics of the New Right, made famous by Margaret Thatcher in the UK and Ronald Reagan in the USA.

Party List

This voting system involves voters choosing a party rather than an individual candidate; when the votes have been counted, seats are allocated to parties based on the proportion of votes received. The representatives are selected from lists drawn up by the parties. It is considered to be a proportional system.

Patriarchy

A patriarchal society is a male-dominated society. Feminists argue that modern society is still characterised by patriarchy.

Referendum

A referendum is a vote on a single question (normally a "yes" or "no" question). At the time of writing, there have been two national referendums in the UK (1975 on EU membership and 2011 on whether to change the voting system to AV) but there have been many more local and regional referendums, including those on devolution to Scotland, Wales and Northern Ireland and also on issues such as whether to have elected mayors. Some countries have many more referendums than the UK.

Rendition

Rendition or "extraorinary rendition" is a term used for transporting prisoners to a different country, often one with different approaches to human rights. For example, it was found that the US government rendered terror suspects to states where torture was widely used, via secret flights.

Rights

Rights are principles of *freedom* or *entitlement*. They might be *civil rights* which we enjoy because we are citizens and come alongside certain responsibilities of citizenship, or they might be *human rights* or *universal rights* which it is suggested that all human beings should enjoy, regardless of citizenship.

Royal Assent

When a bill has passed through all the legislative stages in the Houses of Parliament it then must be signed by the Queen – this is called Royal Assent. Unlike a President, who might chose to veto a new law, the monarch always signs every piece of legislation, so this is really a symbolic gesture.

Sanctions
Sometimes economic sanctions are placed on a country to try and put pressure on it to change certain positions or policies. For example, for many years there were sanctions placed on Iraq to try and impact on its ability to rearm after the Gulf War. A criticism of economic sanctions is that it often most effects the general population rather than the leaders.

Single Transferable Vote
STV is a voting system used in several countries and widely considered to be the one that produces the most *proportional* result. It is however a rather complex system where people rank their preferred candidates who need to reach a quota of votes in order to be elected to multi-member constituencies.

Simple Plurality (See *First Past the Post*)

Social Democracy
Social democracy is, today, generally used to refer to the moderate form of socialism prevalent in many European countries, such as the UK Labour Party. It differs from traditional socialism in that it simply aims to improve social conditions in a capitalist system rather than to replace capitalism with an entirely new economic system.

Socialism
Traditionally, socialism referred to an alternative system to capitalism (and the political ideology that supported this) – one based on collectivism and redistrubtion of wealth. Today, the terms socialism and social democracy are used almost interchangeably and many socialist parties (e.g. the UK Labour Party) do not propose getting rid of capitalism.

Supplementary Vote
This is a voting system which is very similar to AV but is used to elected individuals to position like leader of the Labour Party or London Mayor rather than MPs.

Supreme Court
The UK Supreme Court began work in 2009 replacing the Law Lords as the highest court of appeal in the UK. Unlike supreme courts elsewhere (such as the USA) the UK court has quite limited powers of judicial review, but it can conclude that some legislation is incompatible with the Human Rights Act (not automatically overturning the legislation).

UN

The United Nations is an international organisation through which all the governments in the world coordinate shared positions on some key issues. It was established following the Second World War in an attempt to prevent future global conflicts.

Urbanisation

Urbanisation refers to the development of towns and cities. In developing countries it refers to the flight of people from rural areas to seek work in urban areas and often involves the development of shanty towns and slums. It often comes hand-in-hand with *industrialisation*.

White Collar Crime

This term refers to crime committed by middle-class people. Of course this could be any crime, but is often particularly associated with crimes like fraud, embezzlement, etc.

MODEL ANSWER PLANS

In this section, we will take one 25 mark question from exam-style questions in each of the sections above and produce a detailed plan.

After reading these plans, you should be able to use this book (together with your plans, etc.) to produce similar plans for all the other questions.

Crime, Justice & Punishment: Question 02

"There is no such thing as a typical criminal". What is this question really after? It's all about *who* commits crimes, and this is where you can bring in your knowledge about criminality and certain social groups, and about crime statistics. You would consider the idea of a "typical criminal" in relation to:

Age
Ethnicity
Class
Gender

In each case, statistics appear to show those who would be mostly likely to commit crimes. You should consider whether the statistics reflect reality (and in which case, why) or whether the statistics are misleading for some reason and, again, if so why.

Introduction: Summarize the thought-process above! Your introduction should "decode the question" (i.e. get to the meat of what it is really asking) and set out how your argument is going to develop.

Main body: There are a few different ways you could tackle this essay. You could put forward that there *is* such a thing as the "typical criminal" (at least statistically) and perhaps even describe him (and it would be a him). You could then examine all the evidence that suggests that this is the case, followed by the evidence that it isn't the case at all.

Alternatively – and I think this is the way I would choose to do it – you could evaluate the issue "category by category". Let's go with that approach here:

Age – Criminals are likely to be young adults, according to statistics. Of course, this is particularly true of certain types of crime, particular "anti-social behaviour" of one sort or another. Young adults are more likely to be out and about at night, in groups (link to *sub-cultural theory*?), possibly under the influence of alcohol, etc. It is also the case that the police particularly patrol town centres at night, so perhaps it is just that young people's crimes are more likely to be observed, detected, reported, etc.

Of course, it is also possible that older criminals have just got better at it and are therefore more likely to get away with it!

Ethnicity – Statistics suggest that people from some ethnic backgrounds are more likely to commit crime than others. Black people are significantly over-represented in the prison population, for example. Again you would divide this into considering reasons for this if it reflects reality but also considering reasons why the statistics might be misleading.

True – Overlap between some ethnicities and poverty/social exclusion/ link to subcultures, etc? The latter could link to "gang culture"? Impact of labelling and "self-fulfilling prophesy"?

Misleading – Police racism? Concentration of police resources in certain neighbourhoods?

Class – Pretty much identical to the ethnicity section, only different examples. Could refer to Merton's strain theory and specific subcultural theories but also to Marxist theories of crime.

Gender – Again it's the same debate between whether the statistical differences reflect reality or are misleading. See section in book for detailed discussion of this.

Conclusion: You would obviously reach a conclusion of your own, following logically from what went before. A "sitting on the fence" conclusion would be perfectly acceptable – i.e. for various reasons some people are more likely to commit crimes than others: an old white upper-middle-class woman is less likely to commit a crime than a young, black working-class man, but statistics probably exaggerate the extent to which this is true.

How would you get the marks? *AO1 marks* come from the specific content you include, the theories you mention, any examples you use. *AO2 marks* come from the argument. In this example you would have been evaluating throughout. *AO3 marks* come from your communication skills – the extent to which you structure a good essay and also from your use of appropriate terminology. Talk about *subcultural theories, Marxism, chivary thesis, labelling, strain,* etc. *AO4 marks* come from *synthesis*. Most of this happens quite naturally without you having to self-consciously flag up where you have used knowledge from other modules, although it doesn't hurt to make it obvious. Some of the work on discrimination and identity from CIST1 would certainly be relevant in this essay, and you would have brought it in when considering the impact of police racism (for example).

Politics, Power and Participation: Question 06

Assess the view that Britain should reform its electoral system and adopt a system of proportional representation for general elections (25 marks)

Introduction: As usual this is where we "de-code" the question (i.e. break it down to what it is *really* asking) and set out how the argument will develop.

Here you are asked about the current system for general elections in Britain (First Past the Post) and whether it should be changed, to a system of proportional representation. Therefore, the essay should consist of the strengths and weaknesses of First Past the Post, the strengths and weaknesses of proportional systems (such as Single Transferrable Vote and Party List) and also provides an opportunity to consider alternative systems that are either not proportional (e.g. Alternative Vote or Supplementary Vote) or are "hybrid" (e.g. Additional Member System). If you were to consider all of this in this essay, it would be brimming with an impressive amount of knowledge. You could probably get full AO1 marks just comparing First Past the Post with one proportional system, providing you did so effectively, with good examples, etc. But let's really impress the examiner!

Main Body:

First Past the Post (FPTP): Explain it. Why do we use it? In other words, what's good about it? Simple; usually leads to strong, majority government (not in 2010 of course...); constituency link; familiar; tried and tested, etc.

What's wrong with it? Not *proportional*; problems with over-represented winners and under-represented small parties; the issue of "wasted votes". This is all clearly described in the appropriate section of this book.

What are the alternatives? If the main problem with FPTP is that it's not proportional then we should consider a proportional system like Single Transferrable Vote (STV) or Party List.

As with FPTP describe each system and go through its strengths and limitations. Remember to explain where those voting systems are currently used (at least in the UK – if you're aware of how they are used in other countries then include that knowledge by all means – NEVER KEEP KNOWLEDGE A SECRET FROM THE EXAMINERS!)

Keep focused on the question – for each point about these systems explain whether it strengthens or weakens the case for us *reforming* our voting system for general elections.

If you think any of the arguments listed in this book are particularly strong or particularly weak, say so. You should show that you are aware of a range of views but you do not have to be balanced. You can make your own view very apparent if you have one.

Conclusion: As usual, your conclusion is your own and, providing it follows on logically from what has gone before, you can do as you want. Remember that there are AO3 marks available for having a logical conclusion though, so never be tempted not to bother with one. If you have something of a "sitting on the fence" conclusion (there are strengths of FPTP and PR systems, for example) that might be a good opportunity to propose a hybrid system as an alternative and talk about AMS.

Where will you pick up the marks? No excuse not to get full marks for AO1 here. If you give a detailed account of how the different systems work and how they're currently used, you will achieve that. By evaluating each system and carefully focusing that evaluation on the demands of the question, you will pick up the marks you need for AO2. Structure the essay as above and use appropriate terminology like "first past the post", "winner's bonus", "wasted votes", "coalition", "mandate", "quota", "multi-member constituency", "constituency link" and AO3 marks are no problem. In terms of synthesis, you will naturally include (and develop) your general political knowledge from CIST2 in this answer. If you are able to make any international comparisons, then that synthesizes some knowledge that you might have acquired from CIST4 too.

Global Issues: Question 02

"Globalisation has been overwhelmingly positive for the world." Critically evaluate this view (25 marks)

Introduction: This question suggests a traditional approach to the essay – making the case in favour of globalisation and then the case against it (or the other way around if you prefer). A conclusion might find some middle ground or opt for one of the more uncompromising positions if you prefer it. The introduction should include a definition or explanation of globalisation and then an overview of how the argument will develop: between the hyperglobalist view and the pessimistic globalist view. Within the essay it will be possible to talk about traditionalist and transformationalist views too (probably in the conclusion) and bring in a bit of modernisation theory and dependency theory within the hyperglobalist and pessimistic globalist arguments. So, decode the question and set out how the argument will develop, as usual.

Main body:

Consider, when planning, making a little table:

Globalisation has been overwhelmingly positive	Globalisation has been overwhelmingly negative
Economic development; jobs and opportunities; link to modernisation theory and how LEDCs can develop into MEDCs	Really *westernization* and *Americanization*
	MEDCs use global systems to dominate LEDCs and keep them poor (link to dependency theory)
Tolerant global citizens, more knowledgeable of the rest of the world	Cultural homogenization / cultural imperialism
Travel	
	Low pay, sweat shops and modern slavery
Cheap consumer goods (for people in MEDCs at any rate!)	
	Lack of democratic accountability
Cheap labour costs for transnational corporations (TNCs) – be ready for a strong evaluative point here though!	Impossible for local companies in LEDCs to compete with TNCs

Make sure you use examples where you have them. Mention real situations, real companies, real countries.

Conclusion: It is worth mentioning that some people do not believe globalisation is happening at all. "Traditionalists" believe that globalisation is just another name for modern capitalism and nothing very new has happened in last 50 years or so. They otherwise broadly agree with the pessimistic globalists. There are also transformationalists who share some of the concerns of the pessimistics but believe that governments *can* use their powers to minimise the negative aspects of globalisation and embrace the positives. As usual, it is entirely up to you how you conclude this!

Where do you get the marks? An understanding of globalisation and the main theories, along with real examples, will get you the AO1 marks. The big debate at the heart of the essay is where you will pick up the AO2 marks. Your structure and your use of terminlolgy – like "MEDC", "LEDC", "globalists", "Rostow", "Frank", "cultural imperialism", etc. – will get you the AO3 marks. Material on *political globalisation* demonstrates synthesis with CIST3, while you are also likely to make some links with material on *economic power* from CIST2. This will get you your AO3 marks. If you are a Sociology student who has studied global development you will be at a great advantage here; do not be shy about demonstrating your knowledge from those studies!

GENERAL REVISION ADVICE

How do you revise?

If your answer is that you just read through your notes (or read through a textbook or revision guide) then you are not maximising your chances of fulfilling your potential and getting those high grades. That is not to say you will not get a high grade revising that way – some people undoubtedly do – but the revision probably did not play that big a part in getting the grade!

And let's face it, you spend an awfully long time revising, so it makes sense to use that time in the most effective and efficient way possible.

First of all, make sure you have a revision timetable. Teachers will have mentioned it and you might have decided to ignore them! Don't! It's really important to plan when you are going to revise all your subjects and ensure that you give all of them the appropriate amount of time. If you do not do this, then the chances are you will revise for your first exam first, then for your second, etc. potentially leaving you with very little time to revise for some exams.

Timetable "down time" and leisure activities in your revision plan. If you say that you are going to spend every hour of every day revising Global Citizenship, you will not keep to your timetable, and then you might as well not have written one. If you know that you will watch Eastenders, and you do want to go out with your friends on Friday night, then include that in your timetable. You are much more likely to do the two hours you planned after Eastenders if watching it was in your plan!

Revise in an active way. Do something. Reading your notes, or this textbook, might well trigger a few memories and help a little. But the exam is not going to ask you what you can remember about Citizenship. It isn't a trivia quiz. Therefore it is much more useful to revise material in the way that you are going to use it in the exam.

Active Revision Methods:

- *Mindmaps or "Brainstorms"*. Take *either* a topic *or* a question and *mindmap* it. Connect themes, people, facts and arguments to one another across a large, blank sheet of paper.

You might want to do this with notes at first, and later without notes, almost as a test. Through this method, you go over what you have learned (and perhaps test yourself on it) but, almost more importantly, you *make connections* and *see* how things are *connected*. Doing this with past-paper questions is particularly exam-focused revision.

- *Exam practice*. You can't really beat exam practice. Doing exactly what you will eventually have to do in the exam is the best way to prepare for it. It is likely that teachers will be prepared to mark these practice answers, but you can also use the exam board's published mark schemes to mark them yourself.

- *Tests and Quizzes*. If you have read through your notes, do not just assume that you have remembered it. Get other people in your group to quiz you on the relevant topics. Setting questions for others can also be an effective way of going through your notes in an active way.

- *Record your notes*. This is a bit out of leftfield, but you could record yourself reading your notes (or record your teacher talking in a revision session, with their permission!) and listen to these recordings in the car, before you go to bed, in the bath, etc. The repetition *might* help.

- *Condense your notes*. Less unusually, many people re-write their notes. Personally, I can't see much advantage to simply writing the notes again in exactly the same form (although everybody learns things differently) – what might be more useful is to condense notes into "revision guide" form. In other words, take a topic area that might be five or six pages in your notes and try and *condense* it into a single page, including all the essential information.

- *Post-it notes*. Another unusual suggestion that some students have reported favourably is sticking post-it notes all around your room (and possibly your house) with key points, facts and quotations on them. That way, when you get milk from the fridge, you might read the key elements of the European Convention on Human Rights.

Everybody has their own favourite revision techniques. Discuss it with your group – somebody might have one that would really suit you too. Some people colour code all their notes, others just rely on reading the textbook. Everybody is different, but the more active the revision method, and the closer the skill involved is to those needed in the exam, by far the better.

EXAM TECHNIQUES

What do you do in the exam?

Hopefully you didn't answer, "panic!" The first and most important thing is to read the paper very carefully. You should be fully aware of the style of the paper before you get there, but read the instructions again and be clear what you have to do.

Choosing your question pairs

You should begin both exams with a full choice of questions available to you. It is often the case that a 15 mark question is on a different area of the subject to its associated 25 mark question, so there is no benefit to only revising some of the topics.

Initially try and make your choice based on the 25-mark essay questions. This is where the bulk of the marks are located so it makes complete sense to base your choices on these questions. Of course you might like (or dislike!) two 25-mark questions equally and, here, you might use the 15 mark question as a discriminator. However, my general advice would be to choose a pair by the 25-mark question *even if you are quite unhappy with the 15 mark question.*

Answering the questions

Consider the option of answering the higher mark questions first. Providing you number your answer-book properly and clearly there is absolutely no problem with this. People are often scared of doing it, but it is amazing how often people report having run out of time to finish an essay. If you really can't bear to do it, or if you feel like the 15-markers serve as a limbering-up exercise for the big questions, stick to your usual routine. But starting with the longer questions can really help from a time management point of view.

Really important – make a plan. The 25-mark questions, though shorter than A2 questions of the past, should not just be started without a plan. You need to know where you are going and what you are going to try and include. This does not need to be a long, detailed plan. On your answer-book, do a quick "mindmap" or "brainstorm" to ensure that you have remembered all the relevant information. Either "brainstorm" this into "for" and "against" columns (if appropriate) or number the points before you start writing, to show the order you are going to address them in the essay. Consider ticking them off as you have addressed them. Make sure the plan is legible for the examiner to look at should they wish to – you might pick up some marks (as such, do not cross it out; they cannot mark crossed-out work).

Time Management

Time management is really important. It can be very frustrating in some A Level exams, especially at AS, when it seems almost as though the exam is testing how fast students can write, rather than their understanding of the topics. However, with a clear idea of how much time is available for each question, it should be possible to answer these questions with reasonable comfort.

There are eighty marks available, and ninety minutes available in each exam. Assuming it might take approximately five minutes to read the paper and choose the questions (hopefully it might take a little less) you will then have roughly a "mark a minute", followed by five minutes at the end to read through your answers and make necessary corrections and changes. If you tackle both 25-mark questions first, you should have finished the second one when an hour has passed. If you are into the last 25 minutes and you have not started the 15-mark questions, then you are running behind time. Quick measures like this can be very helpful.

If you finish, do not sit back or (worse) leave. Read through what you have written, carefully. You have been writing quickly, so you will *always* have made one or two careless errors, or expressed something in a way that you might like to improve on. Too many students miss out on that important opportunity to improve their work.

Finally, GOOD LUCK!

Lightning Source UK Ltd.
Milton Keynes UK
UKOW07f2341120917
309073UK00004B/205/P